Happy christmas
Dad
'2010'

All my love Karla xx

BOTHAM'S BOOK
OF THE ASHES

BOTHAM'S
BOOK OF THE ASHES

A LIFETIME LOVE AFFAIR WITH CRICKET'S GREATEST RIVALRY

SIR IAN BOTHAM

MAINSTREAM
PUBLISHING

EDINBURGH AND LONDON

First published in Great Britain in 2010 by
MAINSTREAM PUBLISHING COMPANY
(EDINBURGH) LTD
7 Albany Street
Edinburgh EH1 3UG

ISBN 9781845964917

A catalogue record for this book is available
from the British Library

Typeset in Florencesans and Palatino

Printed in Great Britain by
CPI Mackays of Chatham Ltd, Chatham ME5 8TD

1 3 5 7 9 10 8 6 4 2

For Kath and Kate

ACKNOWLEDGEMENTS

A huge thanks to my England teammates, who made Ashes cricket so much fun and so successful for me. To my Aussie opponents, thanks for giving me such a great challenge whenever I walked onto the pitch and, in so many cases, for becoming good friends off it. I've attempted to explain just how much the contests meant to me within these pages, but sometimes words can't express just how good they made me feel. A particular thanks must go to Suggo, Dusty and Vic for a bit of memory-jogging, too.

The support from the English public during those contests was remarkable and it continues to be so to this day, while the Australian fans gave it to us with both barrels until we earned their respect, and that was always possible. I've enjoyed everything that Ashes cricket has had to offer and continue to love the battles that go on without me. I had my time, I loved it and now I relish what I get to watch. Long may that continue.

To Dean 'The Ghost' Wilson, thanks for making this process as painless and enjoyable as possible and for reminding me of some great memories. It has been fun to talk about the old days while watching the new breed go about their work.

To the publishers at Mainstream, thanks for your support and assistance wherever it has been needed, and thank you to my friend and agent Adam Wheatley for always being there.

Finally, thanks to my family, who make it all worthwhile.

CONTENTS

INTRODUCTION

When Ivo Bligh took his England side to Australia in 1882 to compete for 'the Ashes' of English cricket, he could not possibly have imagined the ferocious competition that he was to pioneer, nor the sort of chaps who would be competing for them after him.

Although England and Australia had been playing against each other for six years, this was the first time that they had played since the *Sporting Times*' mock obituary for the game in England, which declared that 'the body will be cremated and the ashes taken to Australia'.

And from the moment Florence Morphy – the future Mrs Bligh – and a group of Melbourne women presented the captain with an urn containing the burned remnants of a set of bails, or perhaps a lady's veil, the Ashes was born.

Ashes cricket means something very special to me for many reasons. It is full of history and tradition. It is England against Australia, and that brings with it a certain amount of emotional fanaticism. It is not just about what happens on the field; it stirs up a relationship between the two countries that goes back to the days when we were the Poms and they were the convicts.

The Aussies will tell you they were the lucky ones, being sent to a place full of sunshine and beaches while we were left behind in a grey, wet and cold country to sip warm beer, but the truth is that whichever nation holds the urn automatically gets the upper hand on the other.

For English and Australian cricketers, it always has been and always will be the ultimate test. It means more than any other series, and it affects the nation like no other. Playing India or South Africa is plenty to get excited about and might even present a tougher purely cricketing challenge than playing Australia at times, but nothing gets the pulse racing like an Ashes series, and that's true for both countries.

It is a relationship that has developed over time into a bit of a sibling rivalry. Both sides are desperate to get one over on their oldest foe and will do whatever they can to make that happen and earn the bragging rights for another couple of years, but it isn't done with any nastiness or vindictiveness. The Ashes is always contested in a competitive and full-blooded way, but never to an over-the-top degree. It is still sport after all, not life or death – although sometimes it feels that way.

Of course there have been times when things have become a little tasty on the field (and I'll be taking you through some of that action in this book), but that is only because it does mean an awful lot to the guys playing out in the middle as well as the fans around the boundary. However, I can honestly say, hand on heart, that it has never spoiled what is essentially a contest that is a joy to play in and watch. It is a series that enriches both countries and that is what makes it so special.

I totally relished the matches and the series I played against Australia, and it is fair to say that my cricketing career will always be closely associated with the Ashes, but it has run deeper for me than just the numbers and stats that the cricket geeks of this world like to pore over.

The Ashes has provided me with some of the most fantastic memories a man can have. I have made some of the greatest friends in my life through Ashes cricket and I have managed to fall in love with a country other than my own. Along the way, I like to think that I've provided cricket fans with a bit of swashbuckling entertainment at times, and, as an avid Ashes watcher in my youth and now as a commentator, I've been lucky to see plenty of that from other players up close.

There have been periods when the pendulum has swung one way and then the other, but throughout the ages there is nothing that gets the competitive juices flowing like an Ashes series and that always makes it a little unpredictable.

It is also why the grounds are full, why the back pages of the newspapers are devoted to it and why, no matter what changes in the world of cricket, the Ashes remains the contest everybody wants to be a part of.

In these pages, I'll take you through a lifetime's passion, from my earliest days as a cricket fan and watching the likes of Ken Barrington and Colin Cowdrey stick it to the Aussies to my debut in 1977, onwards and upwards through 1981 – although it wasn't all plain sailing that year! – and then to my favourite tour of them all, to Australia in 1986–87. Beyond my days as a player, I've forced myself to look a little closer at the 16-year gap England suffered before getting their hands on the urn in 2005 – and if any series captivated what the Ashes is all about, it was that one.

The future of cricket seems so uncertain at times, with the advent of Twenty20 and the Indian Premier League. There is a very real danger that Test cricket could get left behind in the rush for the wealth and riches that the shorter forms of the game have to offer. However, I can say with some confidence that none of it will ever replace the Ashes and I hope to show you here why I feel that way.

The Ashes has meant the world to me in my life and I hope it has meant something to you in yours. I owe a great deal to this contest, both on and off the field.

EARLY DAYS

I first became aware of the Ashes the day I was born. I'm pretty sure I came charging out of the womb ready to tear in at an Aussie batsman and give him what for; luckily for the Aussies, my umbilical cord held me back and it was to be another 20 years before I got my first crack at them on the field!

In all seriousness, my earliest days as a sports-mad kid were spent trying to be the next Bobby Charlton or Bobby Moore. Football was my first love and although I didn't quite manage to graduate past the English Third Division with Scunthorpe, it was the game I wanted to triumph at. That was, of course, until I tried my hand at cricket and discovered that not only did I have a touch of talent for the game but I also rather enjoyed it and the unique battles it creates between bowler, batsman and fielder.

I knew the Ashes was special because when the team were on tour Down Under we used to get half an hour's highlights at around 11 p.m. That was way past my bedtime when I was a young lad, but my parents would let me stay up to watch when it was on, because I was so transfixed by cricket.

Thinking about it now and being involved in television these days as a commentator, they were pretty poor highlights compared to the incredible pictures we get now, but they were so important. You were usually a day or maybe two behind because of the time difference and you had to try to pick out the players and the ball in these grainy images, but, of course, it was all you had so you enjoyed it at the time. Obviously, things are different now and you get to see absolutely everything in real time, but back then it was about crouching in front of the TV in my pyjamas watching and dreaming of one day being involved.

I first really took an interest in cricket at the age of about six or seven and my love for the game steadily grew as I got older and stronger and realised that it was a game I could play reasonably successfully. I would play plenty of football at school and in the parks as a youngster in the winter and then in the summer, with the encouragement of my dad, Les, and a schoolmaster called Mr Hibbitt, I would turn to cricket, like most young boys did. My ability meant that I could get into school teams earlier than the other boys in my year. By the time I was turning out for the Under-11 side as a nine year old, I was easily outscoring the older boys in the side and it was clear I was taking my first formative steps towards a cricketing career.

Off the field, Kenny Barrington was my first Ashes hero, along with a remarkable bowler called Fred Trueman. I was entranced by the way Fred would charge in to bowl, letting rip with the ball, which looked like it travelled as fast as a bullet, before trudging back to his mark, folding up his sleeve as he went. I used to practise rolling up my sleeves as a kid; thankfully, short-sleeved T-shirts were the norm by the time I was playing most of my cricket professionally.

The thing is, there wasn't actually that much coverage of cricket and Ashes cricket on TV in those days and what you got was only really a glimpse into what was happening. I can still see that chicken – or was it a cockerel? – popping up on the screen heralding the Pathé newsreel that would provide just a taste of what was going on. The way you really found out about your cricketing heroes was through reading the newspapers, and that was just about the only thing I did read as a lad. I can't say that I've ever been a huge fan of reading novels, but if you gave me a paper detailing the latest heroics of England's cricketers in the Ashes, then I'd be all over it.

Things are different today because you get to see so much of what goes on, from the players arriving at airports with intrepid journalists like Tim Abraham thrusting a microphone in Ricky Ponting's face to the latest technology, such as a stump cam that pretty much gives you the batsman's view of the bowler running in. There was nothing of the sort when I was a lad, so if you wanted to see the Australians arriving, you had to get yourself down to the docks and watch them step off the boat – and plenty of people did just that.

Times change and technology has had its impact, but one thing that has remained the same is the extra level of excitement when the Australians come over. I didn't really know what it was all about at the time and when I asked my dad about it he told me something about an urn and Bodyline and convicts, but it all went flying over my head. I had the nickname 'Bungalow' as a young player, so, with nothing upstairs, it is unsurprising that I didn't quite get it to begin with.

The Ashes started to click for me in 1964, when I was eight. I remember looking forward to the series that summer but being disappointed by the weather and some of the cricket on display.

England had not won the Ashes since 1956, the year after I was born, and after two defeats and a draw for the Aussies to retain them, this summer was billed as the perfect chance for England to get them back. Looking back on it now, I realise that I knew something important was supposed to be happening that year because my dad was constantly talking about it and telling me how, without Richie Benaud, Australia were likely to struggle. Of course, I know Richie well now, but in those days his position as one of the finest leg-spinners and captains in the game had really passed me by, as most things did!

Anyway, I do remember being excited by the contest and, through listening to the odd piece of commentary on the radio and having my dad read various bits in the paper to me, I followed that series, and I feel sure that it sowed in me a seed of determination to succeed against Australia that blossomed as I grew older.

The first two matches were badly interrupted by rain and even though England enjoyed the upper hand in both games, there just wasn't enough time for them to force a result.

The weather held firm for the third Test, though, and just like in the Ashes of 2009, the match in Leeds produced England's worst performance of the summer. Headingley is a curious ground when it comes to Ashes cricket. Rarely has there been a dull bore draw there with nothing happening. For some reason, it seems to have created mayhem for both sides over the years and, since Yorkshire is so proud of its cricketing heritage, I suppose it is only fitting that Leeds should have been home to some of the most memorable Ashes contests.

In any case, England came unstuck and lost by seven wickets, thanks largely to a big hundred from Peter Burge, who went on to become an ICC match referee. I can remember that game distinctly for two reasons. First, I recall just how disappointed I was that England had lost. All the talk about it being a great chance to regain the Ashes had eventually got through to me and I was expecting to see English success, not defeat. Because my expectations weren't met in that game, I was very upset about it. Second, my favourite player of that era, Kenny Barrington, very nearly saved the game for England, but his wicket towards the end of the fourth day effectively gave Australia the breakthrough they needed to go on and win.

When Kenny was out for 85, England were 156–4 and had a lead of 35. On the last day, England's remaining 6 wickets added just another 73 and Australia chased down their target of 109 with ease.

From that point on, I was only interested in England getting their own back and followed the fourth and fifth Tests much more closely. The fourth was probably the most boring game of cricket the two sides have ever played against each other. Australia were desperate to hold on to their lead. Bobby Simpson, their skipper, won the toss and batted England out of the game with 311 for himself and 656–8 declared. They were still bloody well batting midway through the third day! England had no real chance of doing anything in the game and a draw was inevitable, the only highlight being a big double ton for my hero Kenny, who made 256. It was a defiant knock, as so many of his were, that simply said, 'I'm not going to dance to your tune and if you want to get me out, you'd better try harder.'

That was the thing that I loved about Kenny. To me, he was the typical bulldog Englishman who didn't give the opposition an inch but was a real gentleman with it. He would stride out to the crease, chest out, chin up, and the opposition knew they were in for a battle. In his later years, as an England coach and manager, he would have a big influence on me and we became firm friends. I always looked up to him, throughout my career, and it was just a sad, sad day when he passed away on tour to the Caribbean in 1981, aged just 50.

It was on to the fifth and final Test. England could now only draw the series, which meant the Ashes stayed with the Aussies, although I didn't quite get that at the time. I thought the Ashes went to the team that won them and that if nobody won them, they just kind of stayed in limbo somewhere.

I had no idea what the Ashes actually were at that time, either. I presumed it was some magnificent trophy, like the FA Cup. As I've since discovered, not many people do know just how small the Ashes urn itself is and people are often quite surprised when they see it up close for the first time. The curators of the MCC Museum at Lord's must be fed up of hearing the words 'But I thought it would be bigger than that!' as tourists flock to the home of cricket to see it.

England lost a series they were expected to win and from that moment on my desire to beat Australia was set in stone. It was to be years later before I got my first real exposure to the Aussies, and it was something I wouldn't forget.

UP CLOSE AND PERSONAL

They say you never forget your first time and I think that is definitely true for me. Watching your first live Ashes match is something truly special and, in my case, getting to see the Aussies play England at Lord's in 1972 was an absolute pleasure, even though a certain Bob Massie had the best debut anyone could wish for and took 16 wickets to square the series for Australia.

By that stage, I was in my second summer on the Lord's groundstaff and one of the duties of the young lads in those days was to take the scorecards around the ground from where they were printed to the various kiosks and sell them. You also had to sell the cushions for the seats to the punters; those plastic Lord's folding seats can be a little bit numbing if you're sat there for the day. One of the other jobs was to help out in some of the bars, which I was a dab hand at, as I'm sure you would have guessed! But on this day at Lord's, it was the second Ashes Test of the summer and I couldn't wait to watch the action.

Obviously, I was really into my cricket by then, and with England having finally regained the Ashes for the first time in my lifetime in the previous series Down Under, I was really up for this one. What was more, my dreams of playing in the contest were starting to seem more and more realistic by this time.

Having sold my cushions and done my chores for the day, I settled down on the grass in front of the Warner Stand with a few of the other groundstaff lads, like my mate Rodney Ontong, and we just soaked it all up. The buzz around the place was like nothing else I'd experienced before. England had won the first Test up in Manchester and the atmosphere was electric.

England held the Ashes, having won them in a tasty series Down Under in 1970–71 with Ray Illingworth as captain. That was probably his finest hour as skipper for England; he was defiant, he was bold and he was a pain in the backside for the Aussies. His decision to take the players off after John Snow got into a bust-up with a few fans on the boundary was typical of the no-nonsense approach he had to his cricket and the loyalty he showed towards his players. I'm not sure how well Illy and I would have got on in the same side, but I'd like to think that we would have respected each other as cricketers and would have rubbed along well enough.

Anyway, back to 1972 and Lord's. England won the toss and chose to bat, and I must admit I wasn't in a mad rush to watch 'Fiery' Geoff Boycott opening the batting, because I reckoned he just might be there all day grinding out another of his patient hundreds. The man I was very keen to see, though, was D.K. Lillee – to my mind, the greatest fast bowler of the lot.

At that stage, I had yet to see him bowl in a Test match at first hand, but I had heard a fair bit about him and the word around the cricket world was that he would break a few records in his time. I got to see him in the nets before the game, but he was hardly going full tilt.

The first morning of a Lord's Test match is bound to bring out something special, as I'm sure Steve Harmison of the recent vintage would testify. So there I was watching Lillee tear in and test out Boycott and John Edrich, and, boy, he was quick in those days.

DK obviously slowed down a touch as he got older and got more control over his swing and seam movement, but 18 months into his Test career he was lightning. England's openers seemed to play him pretty well, though, and the bloke causing the real problems was Massie on debut.

Lillee had made his debut against England in the penultimate match of that 1970–71 tour and announced himself with 5–84 (I think all the best bowlers take exactly five wickets in their debut innings). Massie conceded exactly the same amount of runs as Lillee at Lord's, only he took three more wickets than him and walked off the hallowed turf with 8–84 to have his name etched up on the honours board in the dressing-room.

Massie swung it this way and that from over and round the wicket. It really was a masterclass that none of England's batsmen could cope with. The middle and lower order all got starts and Tony Greig picked up a fifty, but the way Massie was swinging that ball I don't think anyone ever really felt like they were in against him.

When England came to bowl, there were hopes that one of the Johns, Snow or Price, could do the same thing, but it didn't quite work out like that. John Snow did pick up a five-fer, but he had to work much harder for it as the Chappell brothers took the game away from England. Greg Chappell would go on to be one of the game's great batsmen and he showed his class on plenty of occasions in Ashes cricket. This was another of those times as he hit 131 to back up Massie's bowling.

I thought surely things would be different second time around when England batted, but no, Massie's dream debut was only halfway through and he destroyed our batsmen for a second time in the match. In fact, this was even more ruthless as he took 8–53. I can remember the slips having a great time of it, with edges flying this way and that, and thinking to myself that was the place to field. Throughout my career, I used my big hands to great effect in the slips, and when a bowler is on song getting regular edges there is no better place to be. Once again, I wanted to be in the thick of the action and usually that is where the slips get involved.

For Massie, it seemed that every time a batsman hit the ball it went in the air and every time it went in the air someone caught it. The ball was hooping round corners again and the game was up for England.

As it turned out, that was a bit of a freak performance, really. Massie only went on to play five more Test matches, and three of those were in that series. His star just burned too brightly too quickly and before he knew it his Test career was over, nine months later.

I've heard him talk about why his career was so short after a blistering start like that and he says that the weight of expectation on him after that first Test match was so great that he struggled to deal with it. He took a few more wickets in helpful conditions in England, but when he got back home and the ball didn't want to swing as much for him, he really lost his way.

Also, the home fans hadn't seen this guy bowl for Australia yet. They'd just heard about this young bloke who'd taken 16 wickets on debut and must be a terrific bowler. So when he pitched up and didn't do much at home, I think they turned on him a little bit, and that would have been hard to cope with. The Australian sporting public can be extremely tough on sportsmen and women, even when they come from the same shores as them.

A few Aussie sportsmen have told me that when you're good they love you to death and there is no better crowd to play in front of than an Australian one willing you on. But you've got to perform. They know their sport inside out and if you dip below a certain level, after a while they will turn on you and there is no love lost. They are only interested in a team of winners and if you're not pulling your weight, then they want to see someone who will.

As a Pom trying to nick the Ashes away from them, you expect, embrace and almost come to love the abuse and the banter you get from a hostile Aussie crowd, but it must be twice as hard to take when they're your own fans. When your confidence is down, you go searching for the magic balls and you go searching for that elusive swing and, of course, the more you go looking for them, the harder they are to find.

Massie's career might have stalled the moment he walked up the pavilion steps at Lord's for the last time in the match, but his performance over four days there was to my mind the finest example of swing bowling I have ever seen in Ashes cricket and probably in world cricket full stop. Nothing can take that away from him, and it doesn't matter whether he did it once or a thousand times; the fact is that in 1972 at Lord's Bob Massie was the king of swing and his sixteen scalps gave Australia an eight-wicket win and got them right back into the series.

Even though England lost that match, I was hooked on these Ashes contests and I knew I wanted to get involved at some stage. But if I'm honest, it didn't become a burning desire of mine above all other things. It was there in the background, but I also knew that if I succeeded in the games in front of me, progress should take care of itself. I say 'should' because along the way I had more than my fair share of run-ins with authority and selectors, which meant that my path to England and Ashes cricket wasn't perhaps as smooth as it could have been.

That summer, though, I only played fitfully for Somerset Under-25s. Inspired by Massie's performance, I left London a couple of days later and found myself playing against Gloucestershire in Bristol. I was up against people like Zaheer Abbas, the great Pakistani batsman, and David Graveney, who went on to be my captain at Durham at the end of my career and then England's chairman of selectors during their most successful period in recent years.

Obviously, I thought anything Massie can do, I can do better and anything Chappell can do I can do best . . . No, I can't! Figures of 1–34 and a score of five were hardly match-winning stuff as we were stuffed by seven wickets. Never mind, back to London for more chores and to learn about life and the game.

The rest of that summer was dominated by the Ashes as it see-sawed this way and that. A draw at Trent Bridge was followed by a hammering for the Aussies at Headingley, thanks to a ten-wicket haul from Derek Underwood. He really was a master of slow left-arm bowling and was the best English spinner I've seen in operation.

That nine-wicket victory meant England couldn't lose the Ashes, although they could draw the series at the Oval. Unlike in 1964, when I didn't quite understand the retaining side of things, I knew that England would hold on to that little trophy because of the win at Headingley, and it was soon after that game that I actually went to see the urn for the very first time.

I was so caught up in my own existence as a cricketer in those days that even though the urn lived at the same place I did, I hadn't actually gone to see it yet. Terrible, I know, but it just wasn't on my radar at the time, and although the Lord's museum curator had invited me in to see the greatest prize in the game, I hadn't taken him up on his offer. Until now.

I popped in to the MCC Museum one afternoon following a boring net session, had a look at the ultimate prize in the game, as far as I'm concerned, and thought 'Christ, I thought it would be bigger than that!' By that stage, I knew it was small, but I was still taken by surprise at just how small it was.

What I did know, though, was that the urn represented the biggest thing in cricket, from my and every Englishman's and Australian's perspective. One-day cricket was still in its infancy and there wouldn't be a World Cup until the summer of 1975, so the Ashes was the definitive trophy. I still believe that to be the case more than 30 years on.

Over the course of a year, the cricket world is littered with more games than the Summer and Winter Olympics combined. In fact, I don't even know what the cricket seasons in the various countries are any more, because there are matches being played 12 months of the year and more often than not they involve England. Our players play too much cricket at what is supposed to be the highest level, and it means that it is nigh on impossible to be at your best when the big challenges come along. I'm all in favour of our players playing the game, but I think international cricketers are being asked to operate at top capacity far too much.

I'm a firm believer in a bowler bowling lots of overs to get himself in top condition, but it is the type of overs that worries me. When I played the game, you could bowl yourself into form and fitness with your county and then by the time the internationals came along you were raring to go, and because there weren't as many England games as there are now, you could peak when it mattered. Nowadays, the players are being asked to peak all the time and that is causing stresses and strains and lots of injuries. The players then get themselves in the gym to try to become fit and strong to bowl, but that is not the same as bowling fit, so they end up breaking down again. It is a vicious cycle that the game has got itself into at the moment and it is hard to see how they will get out of it, unless they reduce the amount of international cricket being played, which is a bit like asking a tubby kid to give back half his bag of sweets: it ain't going to happen.

Anyway, by the end of 1972 I was hooked on Ashes cricket. I had seen enough to know that the Ashes was the premier contest in the game and that it also meant more than any other. What I still didn't know was whether I would ever get to play in it.

My time on the groundstaff had been OK, but I had probably got on the wrong side of the coach, Len Muncer, a few too many times to be able to call it a great summer. He was a bit of a stern man who didn't really take to my overly confident style and we clashed on a few occasions. Still, I was invited back for 1973 to continue my cricketing education, although, thanks to more opportunities in the Somerset 2nd XI, I was rarely there.

Now, I know this book is all about the Ashes and my relationship with it. However, two things happened in 1974 that had nothing to do with that famous contest but a lot to do with my future, and it would be wrong of me to go on without mentioning them.

At the start of that summer, it was clear I would be given my chance to make a real go of a career in cricket. Somerset had doubled my annual wage to around £500 and I knew things would be expected of me on the field.

I also had a new flatmate at the start of that season, by the name of Viv Richards. I mention this because sharing that flat was where our lifelong friendship was sealed. We had already played together for Somerset Under-25s a couple of years previously and got on well, but during this period we formed a bond that would never be broken. The fact that both he and I have gone on to make successes of our cricketing lives, culminating in knighthoods for the pair of us, is something that is not lost on me. I still find it hard to believe that these two youngsters who had the world before them would go on to achieve what they did, but it happened and I'm incredibly proud to call Viv, or 'Smokes', a true friend.

The second and more important major thing to happen to me that year was meeting my wife, Kath, after a Benson & Hedges Cup semi-final against Leicestershire. Her parents were good friends with Brian Close, who was in fact her godfather. When he invited them to watch the game that day, little did everyone know just how their lives would be turned upside down by yours truly.

Kath and I have come through a tumultuous life together and are stronger now than we have ever been. We were young at just 18 and 19 when I announced to her that we would get married. Not exactly the most romantic of ways to do it, but it worked.

Over the years, we have been through an awful lot together and, thanks largely to her, we have come out the other side. My life with her and our kids and grandchildren up in North Yorkshire couldn't be better.

Having convinced everyone, including Closey, that we actually were serious about our marriage plans, my attentions turned back to cricket in the summer of 1975 and that was where they were to stay for the foreseeable future as I aimed to establish myself as one of the first names on the Somerset team sheet.

Part of that process was to play and impress against the touring sides. Due to a hastily arranged tour, it was Australia who came to England unexpectedly to compete for the Ashes again and I got my first taste of on-field Aussie competition.

OPENING EXCHANGES

I was settled into my career path at Somerset and was fully focused on continuing to establish myself as a first-team cricketer, so it didn't really matter to me who I was playing against as long as I was playing.

In years to come, I would take a bit more interest in which teams were touring England, knowing that I'd be involved and wanting to find out what sort of challenges might be coming my way. I wasn't a huge one for the sort of analysis and homework that is done these days by international teams; I tended to work it out for myself when I was out in the middle. But I suppose it did help me to make mental notes about who we would be playing and what I might like to work on.

In the case of 1975, the Australians had been asked to tour England just a few months in advance, while the Ashes trip to Oz had been going on, so there was no real time to get excited or flustered about it.

Obviously, having broken into the Somerset side the year before, this was a touch too soon for me to be thinking about England honours, but I had already started to think that I would be going all the way. It was more a question of when, in my mind, rather than if, even at that stage.

What I did know, though, was that when the Australians came through Taunton in August, I would be ready for them. Or at least I hoped I would be ready for them; what actually happened was somewhat different from my later performances in matches against the Aussies.

This was an Australian side that had just given England what for Down Under in 1974–75 using the twin spearheads Dennis Lillee and Jeff Thomson to full effect, hitting stumps, helmets and one or two other places along the way – just ask David 'Bumble' Lloyd. Bumble has been a good mate of mine for a long time now and although our England careers never overlapped, our commentary careers will be forever intertwined. It is always a pleasure to be in the box with him – and funnily enough that is exactly where Thommo got him!

Bumble is getting more and more eccentric as the years go by and I do wonder whether it all stems from his one and only Ashes series, in which he was given a bit of a rough time by the meanest fast-bowling duo the world has seen. There is no doubt that he was on the receiving end of a ferocious assault at Perth during that series in Australia, but he can finally talk about it now without tears welling up in his eyes.

He strode out to the wicket in Perth, which in those days was just about the fastest pitch in the world, to face Lillee and Thomson, who both had a point to prove. Thommo hadn't really shown what he was capable of before this series, while there had been some doubt over whether Lillee still had the pace of his early days. In both cases, they got their point across.

Poor old Bumble faced up to Thommo. Steaming in and with his javelin-like style of bowling, he speared one straight into Bumble's nether regions and he was done for. The box he was wearing was not only bent inwards but it had cracked too, and for the only time I can remember hearing about, somehow the part that should have been behind the box was out in front – utter agony! As Bumble waddled off the field with tears justifiably streaming down his cheeks, it was clear what Ashes cricket was all about.

Thommo's famous quote 'I love seeing blood on the pitch' was never more apt than when he was playing against the Poms. He is a fair-dinkum Aussie whom I've got to know well over the years and he makes no apology for the way he went about his cricket, and nor should he. The game is a non-contact sport, but there are plenty of opportunities to do some damage and sometimes you have to be physically brave. It is just another aspect of Test cricket that makes it such a great game. You need skill, talent and ability, but you also need courage, and if you don't have it, guys like Jeff Thomson will soon find you out.

Bumble found out the hard way, but you could never doubt his courage, because the next day he returned to the ground and when it came to his turn to bat, he went straight back into the thick of it, ready to face the onslaught. It didn't take long for him to realise there was no sympathy for him at the WACA. Thommo roared in and pinned him in the throat with a vicious bouncer, and as he was lying down on the ground, the bowler strolled up, picked up the ball and said, 'G'day, you Pommie bastard!' It was tough stuff out there and that is how it always has been and always will be.

Bumble also tells a great story about how, on that same tour in 1974, during the fourth Test in Sydney, Lillee came in to bat and, as England's opening batsman, Bumble thought it best to keep him sweet and not ruffle too many feathers before he was due to bowl. The last thing Bumble needed was an angry opening bowler like Lillee roaring in, especially after the going-over he had given the side in the previous two Tests.

Unfortunately, all-rounder Tony Greig wasn't quite singing from the same hymn sheet and gave Lillee a bouncer that hit him on the elbow and caused a bit of pain. Bumble immediately rushed over to check if he was OK, only for Keith Fletcher, standing at slip, to shout, 'Well done, Greigy! Give 'im another!'

Lillee wasn't having any of that and in a flash turned round and demanded, 'Who said that?'

'I did,' said Fletcher, chest out and staring straight at Lillee.

When the day's play was over and the team got back to their hotel, they were watching TV when Lillee came on and was being interviewed about the current match and series. The interviewer asked him, 'How do you get on with the England team and what sort of blokes are they?'

Lillee thought about it and said, 'The Poms are good sorts. I get on well with them all.' He then leaned into the camera and, staring straight down the lens, he added, 'Except that little weasel Fletcher. I know you are watching, mate, and I will sort you out tomorrow!'

Apparently, all the England players bar Fletcher thought that was hilarious.

When it came for Fletcher to bat the following day, Lillee made sure he had the ball in his hands and gave him a classic barrage of short-pitched and quick stuff. To Fletcher's credit, he played it all pretty well, until one just managed to sneak through his shot and scone him right on the peak of his cap, causing England bowler Geoff Arnold to comment, 'Blimey, he's knocked St George off his 'orse!'

It was more or less carnage for England on that tour as they lost 4–1 to the rampant Australians and, for me, there was a real sense that things might continue that way when a reciprocal tour was arranged for 1975.

As the first-class game against Australia approached, I was feeling in decent form and was loving being a regular part of Somerset's first team. I wanted to play as many games as possible because it meant more chances to show what I could do.

Unfortunately, there appears to be a trend among our counties these days towards fielding experimental teams against the tourists and I think that is a real shame. It short-changes the crowd who come to see the international players given a run for their money by their home side, plus it doesn't help England, because there can be no worse feeling for a touring team than to be beaten by a domestic side before an international match. That is the attitude most sides seem to take against England when we tour, and it should be the same for us.

Back in 1975, I was looking forward to playing the Aussies for the first time, although I would have been glad to play the Somerset Farmers Union XI too. I'm not saying it wasn't special to play Australia, it was just that I was so intense with my cricket back then that I just wanted to play. As it was, I would be playing against some truly world-class players over the three days.

D.K. Lillee was a remarkable bowler, so when I saw his name down on the team sheet I was thrilled because it would give me a chance to watch him up close for the second time after Lord's in 1972, and also I quite fancied seeing what he was like to bat against if I got the chance.

The other name in the Aussie side that got my juices flowing was the skipper, Greg Chappell. He really was one of the game's finest batsmen and I was desperate to bowl at him, and as many players like him as possible, to test myself and see just how good I was. If anyone was going to make you look ordinary, it was likely to be Greg Chappell and, as he was a former Somerset player who'd scored a fair few runs and taken plenty of wickets, there was an extra bit of excitement involved with him coming back to his old county.

As it turned out, another special player took the plaudits with the bat: Doug Walters took a classy ton off our bowlers and, despite bowling 21 heartfelt overs, yours truly ended up wicketless in front of the Taunton faithful.

Having declared on 331–7, the Aussies gave us a tricky little session to deal with before the close and unluckily for Brian Rose, who would go on to be chairman of Somerset, he was snaffled by Gary Gilmour.

I'm generally not a big fan of nightwatchmen, but on that day I was asked to do the job and protect Pete 'Dasher' Denning. Personally, I always believed I was a number three anyway, but for some reason others disagreed!

Naturally, I went in to bat and dealt with the last few overs with ease, ending the day eight not out and looking forward to my inevitable hundred that would follow the next day.

Full of optimism and ready to take on Lillee, I resumed my innings and before I could say 'G'day, mate' my stumps had been flattened by Gilmour and I was back in the hutch without adding to my score. Of course, I was upset, but, as it turned out, I had my pads on again before the day was out as we got rolled for just 106 in little more than 30 overs and had to follow on.

I thought I had just been getting my eye in before Gilmour got me in the first innings, so I pleaded with Closey, our captain, to give me another shot at number three. He was having none of it and instead I was back down to my then usual eight. We put up a much better fight second time around and by the end of the second day we had just managed to creep past the Aussie total so they would have to bat again. At 242–5, I was the next man in, and with my old mate Vic Marks at the crease, that could have been at any time!

I'm being a little unfair about Vic, although he won't mind because he is one of the game's genuinely good guys. I played a lot of cricket with him down in Somerset and then with England, especially in the one-day side, and there is no question that he was a very useful all-round cricketer. His off-spinners were usually beautiful, arching deliveries without a hint of pace on them whatsoever, and it was that gentle flight that tricked batsmen into false shots. He used to get hit for his fair share of sixes, like any spinner, but he refused to dart it in at the batsmen, and I liked that. Listeners to *Test Match Special* on the BBC will have become used to his intelligence and thoughtful comments on the game and, of course, that infectious chuckle he has when something tickles his funny bone.

It was quite obvious that we would most likely lose this game at some stage on the third day and, as was often the way in games like these, there was a real festival atmosphere around Taunton. There was a healthy crowd and everyone was in pretty good spirits. I know the Aussies have rightly got a fearsome reputation for sledging, but they also know when to go along with things and add to the fun of the fair, and during the second day's afternoon D.K. Lillee did just that.

Lillee spent many a year steaming in for Australia, but in a tour match he wasn't going to operate at full Ashes tilt. One wag in the crowd, though, dared him to charge in off the long run and shouted, 'Oi, Dennis! I guess the days when you pushed off the sight screen are long gone, then, eh?'

Well, DK didn't need a second invitation. He turned and marched past his small run-up, past his long run-up, carried on until he reached the crowd in front of the old pavilion and then kept on going! He got them to part like Moses and the Red Sea before charging through them and all the way to the wicket, releasing a thunderbolt. It got a great reception from the fans, so he did it again and again, each time chatting with them about what ball he was going to bowl, and they loved him for it.

At the end of the day's play, he sat down in a deckchair out the front and just signed autographs for about an hour. There was quite a queue formed around him, but he just patiently signed away while sipping the mandatory beer. It was all part and parcel of the game for him and he handled it really well. When I became a little bit more well known, I used to struggle with all the attention people wanted from you everywhere you went. If I could have my time again, I probably wouldn't be quite as annoyed by it. Now that I'm a commentator and grandad, I'm much more relaxed about all that and happily sign autographs and have photos taken, because it makes a difference to the people who come up to you.

As we all knew it would, the final day petered out to a nine-wicket defeat for us, but not until I'd had another go at swatting the Aussies around the park. My flashing blade made quite a sound as it met an easy leggie from Jim Higgs; the only problem was that the noise came from the edge as it landed in the hands of the keeper and I was gone for my first (and certainly not last) duck against Australia.

All in all, my first exchange with Australia was a pretty poor one, personally and from a team viewpoint, but I did enjoy it and I couldn't wait for my chance to take them on when they were going full tilt.

At that stage, England were 1–0 down in the Ashes after two matches, with the Aussies having won at Edgbaston and drawn at Lord's. There had been a few changes in the line-up from the previous winter as guys like David Steele and Graham Gooch came into the side in a bid to shore up the batting. It worked. David in particular was a revelation, having been given his chance by new captain Tony Greig, and although he didn't get to three figures in the series, he almost always got a fifty, which was something, and his defiance towards the Aussie pacemen was rewarded with the BBC Sports Personality of the Year award.

At Headingley in the third Test, it was his 92 that ensured Australia would have to chase a record 445 to win on the last day, and at 220–3 on the evening of the fourth there was a real chance that something special might happen at that old ground, especially since the pitch was playing so well. England had a real chance of levelling the series too, and it could have been a great day.

But when it came for the fifth day to start, the pitch would have played anything but well. Some crazy vandals had broken into the ground and dug up parts of the wicket, pouring oil on a length too. It was a shocking protest, made on behalf of some criminal called George Davis, and spoiled the fun for millions of people both in England and Australia. My old adversary Geoff Lawson, who became a pretty handy bowler for the Aussies despite his short fuse, told me that as a schoolkid in 1975 he had studied all day just so that he could stay up to watch the cricket in the evening. Poor Geoff reckons he had never worked so hard in all his life, just so he could watch the cricket with a clear conscience, and then that happened and it was all for nothing. Well, apart from his education, I suppose!

The draw meant that Australia would retain the Ashes regardless of the result in the final Test at the Oval, but England were keen to square what had been a well-fought series. However, just as had happened in 1964, Australia's captain, Ian Chappell, won the toss and batted England out of the game, helping himself to a big hundred along the way. The late, great Bob Woolmer hit a solid ton in England's second innings and the game ended in another draw, giving the Aussies a 1–0 win, which was a much better showing than just a few months earlier Down Under.

As always, it wouldn't be long before the teams locked horns again, and I actually thought my chance to be involved for the first time might come in the Centenary Test in Melbourne at the end of the winter tour in 1976–77, but unfortunately the only chance I got during that match was to be the team dogsbody.

In 1976, things moved along nicely for me both at Somerset and with England as I was picked for my first one-day internationals against the West Indies. I had scored my first hundred for Somerset, was taking plenty of wickets and felt ready for international competition, so at the end of that summer when Tony Greig, the England captain, implied that he would be taking me on tour, I was delighted and ready for it.

When the squad was announced to go to India and to Australia for the Centenary Test, however, I was nowhere to be seen. The selectors had disagreed with Greig and left me at home. I was fuming at that decision, because I had been expecting to go, and to be let down from such a high was hard to take. I sulked about it, really, and was probably a nightmare for Kath to live with.

Just as I had settled in to the winter, I got a call from Donald Carr at the Test and County Cricket Board (TCCB) telling me that I would be going to Australia after all, only not as an England player but as part of the Whitbread young player scholarship, and I would be playing for Melbourne University. I saw this as a mixed blessing. On the one hand, I would be furthering my cricketing education (or at least I thought I would); on the other, I was leaving my young wife behind and the money wasn't exactly enough to support the both of us. Luckily, Kath agreed that I should go after they upped the fee for the trip.

While I was out there, I got to see Australia up close for the first time and I must say it didn't leave the lasting impression on me that it subsequently did. I've grown to love Australia almost as much as I love England, but my first trip wasn't all that great for a few reasons.

On the cricketing side of things, it just didn't really work out for me there, due in part to the weather, which was incredibly wet while I was there, and also because most of the games were more of a social affair than a real test of cricketing ability.

There were the odd words exchanged in games that left me in no doubt that the Aussies liked to play hard and give it to the Poms any which way they could.

INTO THE
DRESSING-ROOM

'**B**otham! Where is my tea?!' 'Botham! Get me the paper!' 'Botham! I need another towel!' 'Botham! Clean up that mess!'

And so it went on for the entirety of the Centenary Test in Melbourne. But I loved it. Not so much the fetching and carrying, which I did plenty of, but being there right in the thick of it as England clashed with Australia at the MCG.

Myself and Graham Stevenson were given the job of looking after the England dressing-room while we were out there in 1977, which was an absolute treat. Even though I had played a couple of one-dayers and was on the cusp of the Test team, I was still young at the time, just 21, and the chance to be amongst the team during the match was something I relished.

I got to see at first hand how these great players got ready for their cricket and how things operated behind the scenes. If this was a place that I wanted to spend much of my time in the future, then it was great to pick up a few tips. It also gave me a chance to have a few beers with the players after the game and get to know them a bit better, which would come in handy if and when I made it to their level.

Before the match, though, I had got myself into the first of many scrapes I would get into on tours while having a 'social drink'. It is something that has become a bit of a household story and the tale has developed over the years through a variety of Chinese whispers, but, as I've said before and will say again, my run-in with Ian Chappell in a Melbourne bar was a matter of honour, plain and simple.

Ian was a bloke I was clearly destined not to get on with, and that is fine by me. I've always been straight up about the things that matter to me, and my country and its people come under that umbrella.

In 1977, Chappell and I had a disagreement during my time with Melbourne University, where, in between games, part of my training and learning would take place as I bowled to the Victoria state players in the nets. The weather wasn't great during my time there and we didn't actually get to play as many matches as I would have liked, but even bowling in the nets was better than twiddling your thumbs and watching the rain fall. It was after one of these net sessions that I went with a few of the Victoria players to the Hilton bar, where I bumped into Chappell.

I was quite happy to mind my own business and enjoy a night out with the guys, while Chappell was busy indulging in his favourite pastime of Pommie-bashing. When he discovered that I was a Pom, that was it. He went into overdrive and was being even louder and ruder about England than before, to the point where it was spoiling the evening for those around him. It didn't matter to me that he was the captain of Australia, I simply asked him to pipe down and stop the abuse. He didn't, so I asked again. After the third time, I'd had enough of his goading and threw a punch.

I wouldn't say that physical violence is necessarily an answer to life's problems, but sometimes there are people in this world who understand nothing else. I should also point out that, as a young provincial lad from Yeovil, I wasn't exactly well versed in the diplomatic tools preferred by the Kofi Annans amongst you. Still, you live and learn, and I can say that I don't normally go for that method of conflict resolution these days. That incident happened more than 30 years ago now, and little has changed between Chappell and me. The fact that it rumbled on a few weeks later during a club match probably didn't help; but he couldn't resist having another verbal pop at me while I had my arm in a sling from injuring it diving in the field. Only 'soft Poms' got injured, according to him. Nowadays, we are often in the same media area of a cricket ground due to our work as commentators, and we have even stayed in the same hotel on occasions, but there is no friendship there. There isn't really much animosity, either. It is just a nothingness; I don't waste my time with him and vice versa. That is just the way it is.

I did make some friends during that period, though, like the English hero of the Centenary Test, Derek Randall. He was just an incredible cricketer who inspired affection in his teammates and irritation in opponents.

I don't think the Australians had ever come across a player quite like him before and I don't think they knew how to handle him. He was always talking to himself when he was batting and in his first Ashes Test he was rabbitting away like nobody's business as Lillee tore in at him and gave him an uncomfortable few overs in the second innings. England had already been bowled out for 95 in the match, so not a great deal was expected second time around, but 'Arkle' put up one hell of a fight and batted brilliantly, despite being hit firmly in the head by a Lillee bouncer.

He and Dennis Amiss were in the process of putting on a partnership of 166 when Lillee sconed him with a bumper and he went down motionless. As everyone gathered around him thinking he might be dead, he stirred, turned to DK and said, 'My, my, Mr Lillee, that was a jolly good ball, that one! Well done!'

Well, DK was completely taken aback by that response but gathered himself quickly enough to turn to his teammates and say, 'Give me the bloody ball and I'll give him another one.'

As it happened, Derek ended up down the other end facing mainly Max Walker, while Dennis had to face up to his namesake and battle his way to 64.

In the end, England's target of 463 was 45 too many and they ended up losing by exactly the same margin as they had done in the first-ever Test 100 years before. Our Sky Sports statistician, Benedict Bermange, would be astonished to hear me trot out a stat like that (he knows I have better things to do with my time than look at facts and figures, and so should he), but this was a quirk of the game that you couldn't fail to notice.

One other thing I did notice during that match was the sheer size of the MCG and the impressive atmosphere. It was to become one of my favourite cricket grounds in the world when I finally got the chance to play there, and being in the dressing-room for that first time filled me with more determination to make sure I would play the next time around.

Walking out onto that turf at the Melbourne Cricket Ground on Boxing Day in front of 100,000 fans desperate to see us fail is the biggest adrenaline buzz I have had in my life. That, for me, is what top-level cricket – indeed, top-level sport – is all about: you walk out there and you're desperate to perform; you're desperate to show everyone what you can do. They've paid their money to come and see you fall flat on your face and to watch their heroes take the mickey out of you. They're not interested in how tough it is for you to be away from home or how everything is stacked against you. And that was always a great incentive to go out and put on a show.

People talk about pressure in sport. What pressure? How can you not want to just get out there and do your stuff? You know you can do it, they know you can do it but will try everything to stop you from performing, so you just lap it up and get on with it. That's not pressure, that's fun. That is the lifeblood of sport, and if you don't like it or find it a bit hard to deal with, well, there are plenty of other things that you could be getting on with. Give me a player who relishes the heat of battle and going toe-to-toe with the opposition over someone who feels the 'pressure' any day of the week – my side will win.

The Centenary Test also taught me something about the nature of Australian sportsmen. They are the toughest, meanest and most wholehearted competitors you will ever play against, but they are also the fairest. I first came to that realisation based on the evidence of what I saw from the players' balcony in Melbourne.

Arkle was batting like a dream and had made 161 when Greg Chappell was bowling and appeared to get him out. The ball nipped back into him, flicked his pad, made a noise and was caught by keeper Rod Marsh. Now, Rod is a guy whom I would get to know very well over the years and he is one of the great men of the game, but back then I only knew him as Australia's teak-tough stumper. The fielders went up and the umpire gave him out, but on getting up off the ground Rod called out for Derek to come back because the ball hadn't carried all the way and had actually bounced in front of him. No one had noticed and no one would have said anything if it hadn't been for Rod's honesty. It was a crucial time in the game and for him to call Arkle back like that was a real sign of class. Everyone in the dressing-room was impressed with that little piece of cricket. They call it 'the Spirit of the Game' these days and I always find it a little bit of a shame that it needs to be formally written down as a preamble to the laws of the game. The players should be well aware of what is right and wrong on a cricket field.

I returned from Australia looking forward to the summer of 1977, first because my son Liam was due to be born at some point in August and also because I felt it could be my time to break into the England Test team for the Ashes series ahead.

I thought my performances with the bat and ball should be enough to get me into the side on merit alone, but, as I'd seen from the selectors' attitude towards me the winter before, there was always a chance that wouldn't be enough.

As it turned out, the fixture list gave me two shots at the Aussies before the main event and, having felt disappointed by my first attempt at making an impression a couple of years beforehand, I was champing at the bit to get stuck in and show what I could do.

There was also a real feeling that I might get a chance in the full side because throughout that winter the Kerry Packer affair involving Tony Greig and a whole raft of the world's best players had been raging, and there was likely to be a changing of the guard in many teams. I wanted to be ready for it if and when it came.

The game this time was at Bath rather than Taunton and it was a ground that I used to enjoy playing at. The crowd were always keen to see us at their out ground and they were quite knowledgeable. By this stage, I was turning in pretty consistent performances, and I wanted to make my mark on the Australians, especially if I was going to have a go against them later in the summer.

We played them pretty early in the season, in May, so the ball was doing a bit throughout, and if it hadn't been for Greg Chappell's 113, we would have rolled them for about 100. As it was, we managed to cruise past their first-innings score of 232 thanks to a wonderful ton from Brian Rose and a cheeky half-century from yours truly. There was no Dennis Lillee on this trip, so there was definitely a sense that you could get yourself in against their attack without encountering a double-pronged pace assault with Thommo at the other end.

Even then, my batting style was well honed: if it was there to be whacked, I'd give it one, and if it wasn't, I'd probably try to give it one anyway! That was certainly the case as I took twenty from one Kerry O'Keefe over. The poor leg-spinner didn't know what hit him. I got to my fifty in just 38 balls and felt I could do anything.

What I was really pleased with, though, was the way I backed up that knock with the ball. By the end of the second day, the Aussies were in a bit of a hole, 4 wickets down and with a lead of just 64, so we knew we had a sniff. On the last day, I managed to capture 4 wickets, including the wicket of skipper Greg Chappell, as we left ourselves a target of 181. Little did Greg or I know that history was to repeat itself later on that year.

Sensing a famous Somerset victory, we went after the runs with real gusto. My old mate Viv was keen to stick one over the Aussies as a taste of what was to come from him against them over the next 15 years or so. I crashed another quick-fire 39 not out to make sure that the celebrations in Bath could start as quickly as possible.

That was my first-ever taste of success over Australia and, boy, did it feel good. It wasn't a Test match, I know, and I'm sure the Australians weren't as pumped up as they would be for England, but when you're out in the middle you forget who you're playing against: as a bowler you want to take wickets and feel in good rhythm, and as a batsman you don't want to get out.

For us to get one over on them was a real achievement, and I've never been one to avoid the bar when my team have just won. I didn't ignore it too much when we lost, either, but at least this was a better excuse. After the heady time we had in Bath, the team and I came back down to earth with a bump in the Benson & Hedges Cup match against Lancashire that followed. We were dealt with by five wickets and I for one came in for a bit of tap.

I had to get that out of my system pretty quickly because just four days later I was up against the Aussies again and this time it was at Lord's for the MCC.

At that stage, I was so pleased to be playing them at the home of cricket. It wasn't until later in my career that I fell out of love with the place as a result of some less than supportive behaviour from the members there. But in 1977, I was back at my old stomping ground as an MCC young cricketer and it was great to be in familiar surroundings with some friendly faces there to greet me.

Perhaps I was a little too enthusiastic and cocksure. After my performance at Bath, I thought I could do anything against this side – and how wrong I was. I took only one wicket as we dismissed them for under 200 only to see us rolled for 136. In their second innings, I picked up a couple, but I also went for a few runs as my attempts at bouncing them out didn't really work too well.

In our second innings, chasing 315 to win, we ended up 79 runs adrift, my contribution being a second duck in three games against the Aussies. This time it was Thommo who did for me, with one of the quickest balls I had faced in my career up to that point. It was clear he had been bowling within himself in Bath and, after getting spanked a bit by me on that day, he decided to let rip. To be honest, I think I did quite well to get a nick on it through to Rod Marsh behind the stumps.

As he ran past me, Thommo made it clear what he thought of my ability when he told me to 'piss off, you useless Pommie bastard'. That comment was to be a recurring theme with him throughout his career, although, to be fair, he often had occasion to use it. Like most of the Aussie players I've got to know over the years, he is a great bloke and someone I could call a friend.

I didn't know it at the time, but playing in that match had a direct influence on my Ashes debut a couple of months later. It was the first time I had played under a man by the name of Mike Brearley, and it was certainly not going to be the last.

Brears would go on to become the finest captain England had seen in a long time and arguably the best ever. He was without question my greatest captain. Without his influence and man-management of me in my earliest days as an England cricketer, things might not quite have gone to plan for me. He was also a more than useful opening and middle-order batsman, which is sometimes forgotten amid all the plaudits he gets for his captaincy. He never quite managed to translate his batting form for Middlesex into big runs for England, but when we needed a steady hand on the tiller he was the calmest, most thoughtful and most respected man around.

His career is forever intertwined with the Ashes, and understandably so; he led England to three series wins over the Aussies in four attempts. And his first was about to start, thanks to the Kerry Packer affair and the sacking of Tony Greig as England captain that summer.

It was a period of unrest around the cricket world due to Packer and, because of Tony, England was right in the thick of it, especially when the court case over restraint of trade was dealt with on our shores. It seemed quite bizarre that an Australian problem should blow up in England like it did, but that's the law for you, and in the end it provided a good result for the players and ultimately the game.

FANTASY TEAM 1

Over the past 35 years or so, I have played in or watched nearly every single Ashes Test match between the two oldest enemies in the game, and I know that for many players their involvement in those contests was the very peak of their career.

An Ashes Test series remains the pinnacle for English and Australian cricketers, and I don't know any player, current or former, who would give that up for anything else in the game. While some of the very best cricketers ever to have played the game, such as Sir Viv Richards and Sachin Tendulkar, have never been able to compete in this series, many of those who have can rightly be considered to be greats of the game.

We all like playing those games where we pick our best imaginary sides to do battle with each other and wonder what might happen, and I'm no different. Within the Fantasy Team chapters of this book I have picked the 11 Englishmen and 11 Australians whom I would love to have seen compete alongside and against each other, and explained my selection.

I have limited myself to those who played with or against me or on whose matches I have commentated; they must also have played a significant role in an Ashes-winning side and their record in Ashes cricket must be impressive. Pretty simple, really, but those criteria help explain why someone as good as Graham Thorpe doesn't get into my side even though he has a very good record against the Aussies.

Hopefully, you will agree with plenty of my picks, but I

expect you'll disagree with others. Either way, I think it is fair to say that if the following 22 players could get out on to a pitch together, it would be one hell of match – and regardless of the result, it would be one hell of a party that followed.

THE OPENERS

CHRIS BROAD

If ever you wanted to meet a cricketer who cared about what he was doing out in the middle, then you need go no further than search out Chris Broad. He cared so much that his passion would often spill over into an explosion out on the field or in the dressing-room, and if there had been the same referees in his day as there are now, he would never have seen a red cent of his match fee. It is why there can be absolutely no question whatsoever that Stuart Broad is the son of Chris. Whenever you see Stuart give it the double teapot or make an angry gesture out in the middle, it is nothing less than what his dad would have taught him. The irony of it all is that Chris is now a match referee himself, and a fairly strict one at that, which is quite beyond me.

He gets into my team, though, based on his incredible performance during our successful 1986–87 tour to Australia. He hit three hundreds throughout the series as we won 2–1 to claim the Ashes for the last time in eighteen long years. He also cracked a brilliant hundred against the Aussies during the Bicentennial Test in Sydney a year later to prove that his golden series wasn't a fluke.

In the dressing-room, Chris was all right, but it is fair to say that when you arrived at a ground you didn't know which Chris you were going to get. Some days, he could be humorous and quite relaxed and at other times he would be dour and grumpy. I think that we all found him to be a complex character. But in Australia in 1986, we had a very happy dressing-room once the international cricket started. When you're winning, it is much easier for players to get on, and I think Chris thrived in that environment.

We also enjoyed it more because we had been written off and I know that Chris certainly relished proving people wrong. Not only was he fuelled by the suggestion in some quarters that he wasn't quite good enough for the highest level, but he also used the slight against the team as a motivating factor. I can remember him coming back into the dressing-room after scoring 162 at Perth in the second Test and demanding, 'Who can't f***ing bat now?!' He loved the satisfaction of proving himself to be such a good player when it mattered most. I still cannot believe he only played twenty-five Test matches in his entire career, despite scoring six Test tons. That goes to show the crazy attitude we had towards selection during the late 1980s and early 1990s.

I can say, as a teammate of his on a fantastic tour of Australia, that he would have been in my team more often than not. I can't say that Chris was a livewire when it came to nights out and the rest of the cricketing social scene, but then I think openers have to be a bit dull to try not to get carried away; when the world's fastest bowlers are fresh and firing at you with a new ball in their hands, you have to be sharp. I look upon openers as a bit like racing drivers, who can be very quiet and reserved off the track so that they can remain focused on it, and I think Broad fits into that category quite nicely – hence the explosions when he got out and could lift the pressure that he had kept under wraps throughout his innings.

BROAD V. AUSTRALIA

Played: 8
Won: 2
Drew: 3
Lost: 3
Runs: 708
Average: 59.00
Centuries: 4
Ashes won: 1986–87

GEOFF BOYCOTT

It didn't matter who we were playing, there was only one thing on Geoff Boycott's mind, and that was runs. Some guys like wine, others like beer and some like food, but the only thing Geoffrey liked was runs, and nothing gave him greater pleasure than to arrive at the ground the next day brandishing the papers to show everyone just how many he had scored.

The beauty of that approach was that he was never fazed by the increased pressure and attention that an Ashes series brought. So many players can succeed when the series is a bit low key, but then they get thrown into a big one against Australia and they freeze for whatever reason. Think Ravi Bopara scoring three successive tons against the West Indies and then being caught in the headlights during the 2009 Ashes. That would never happen to Boycs because he kept everything the same. Don't get me wrong, he loved playing Australia because it was tough and he liked to score tough runs – they meant more to him than anything else – but the numbers on the scorecard came first.

I only played with 'Fiery' towards the tail end of his England career. Although we were two completely different animals, we got on well. He didn't like me taking the mickey and playing jokes on him, but he took it in his stride and gave me the moniker 'Guy the Gorilla', which I suppose got me back for doing things like cutting his ties.

We all know that although Geoff Boycott had a marvellous record as a batsman, he could bore the pants off those watching in the stands; however, that is exactly the reason why I'd want him to open the innings in my team against Australia. As far as I'm concerned, I want my openers to blunt the opposition's opening bowlers. If they score a few runs along the way, then great, but I just don't want to see my middle order having to face a fresh Dennis Lillee. He's got to earn the right to bowl at them and you'd know that Boycs would make him do that. Also, from a bowler's perspective, if I've just been busting a gut to bowl out the opposition and finally get the chance to put my feet up in the changing-room, I don't want to be told I need to get my pads on before I've even cooled down, and that is why Boycs was so important to our team. I wasn't there, but his record on the Ashes tour of 1970–71 was incredible: five fifties and two hundreds in the five Test matches he played. He also picked up another four hundreds on the tour, which showed him to be at the absolute peak of his powers. The partnership he fostered with Brian Luckhurst at the top of the innings was absolutely crucial in the 2–0 win and gave Ray Illingworth a decent start in virtually every match.

Being in the dressing-room to watch him score his hundredth first-class century, against the Aussies at Headingley, was a real thrill for me as a young England player. I looked up to him a lot. When all eyes were on him, he performed. That is what Ashes cricket is about.

BOYCOTT V. AUSTRALIA

> Played: 38
> Won: 13
> Drew: 16
> Lost: 9
> Runs: 2,945
> Average: 47.50
> Centuries: 7
> Ashes won: 1970–71, 1977, 1978–79, 1981

DAVID BOON

I could have chosen any number of tremendous Aussie openers of recent vintage, but David Boon gets my vote because he was the complete package: a remarkably tough, competitive batsman who never gave an inch, he was a bloody fine player and a great bloke with it. If you think of the men who have missed out, like Langer, Hayden and Taylor, it tells you just how highly I rate Boonie. I wonder whether Boonie would get into the Australian side today – not because he wouldn't be good enough, but because he barely got through the training in those days, and I know he wouldn't be a fan of the fitness regime involved in the game now. Much has been made of the record number of tinnies that he quaffed on the flight from Australia to England for the tour in 1989, but what is less well known is that he is still trying to get the three cans he had at the airport to be included in that number.

He might not have liked the training but, boy, could he play cricket, not only as a fantastic batsman who could open the innings or bat at three and give the new ball a thunderous smashing but also as the best short leg I ever saw operate. He had a low centre of gravity, which no doubt helped, but his reactions at dealing with fast bowling translated to his fielding as well, so that he could catch anything that came his way. His catch off Devon Malcolm to give Shane Warne his hat-trick on the 1994–95 tour could not have been pulled off by anyone else.

His batting, though, is why he would be in this team, and the thing that I would have to tell my bowlers is that they'd have no margin for error where he was concerned. He would cut and pull you all day long if you got your length a little wrong or gave him any width whatsoever. I never really enjoyed bowling to short fellas like Boonie because they could take advantage of the usual lengths you would bowl to normal-sized people and play you off the back foot for fun.

I also have a lot of time for what Boonie came and did at Durham after I was finished. He helped get the club going in the right direction and gave it a bit of grit, which is something the people of the North-East have in common with their Antipodean cousins.

On his last Ashes tour, he was immense and helped lay down the platform that Mark Taylor and then Steve Waugh built on. He was particularly important in the Aussie team's bonding sessions post-match when they won a game. They have a tradition that states that no player can leave the dressing-room after a win until the song 'Under the Southern Cross I Stand' has been sung. One member of the team holds the role of leading the team in the song and Boonie was that man in his day. He would make sure everyone was suitably relaxed before bellowing it out, and they loved him for it. I know he really enjoyed it towards the end of his career, largely because there weren't too many chances to sing it in the early days.

BOON V. ENGLAND

Played: 31
Won: 15
Drew: 11
Lost: 5
Runs: 2,237
Average: 45.65
Centuries: 7
Ashes won: 1989, 1990–91, 1993, 1994–95

MICHAEL SLATER

Slats was one of the most exciting and explosive batsmen ever to play the game. You just knew that if he batted for a couple of hours, he would take the game away from you, just like he did to England at Lord's in 1993 and then again in Brisbane in 1994. His 152 in just his second-ever Test match announced him to the world and created an Ashes hero. To do that on the biggest stage of the lot when just 18 months before he wasn't even in the New South Wales side was nothing short of amazing. Following it up with 176 in the return series Down Under to kick things off proved that he wasn't a flash in the pan and that the man from Wagga Wagga was a serious cricketer. And he did it with such speed and in such brutal style that no captain could really contain him. For him to do that as an opener was just remarkable and there is no question that he was a trailblazer.

We are now used to seeing guys like Virender Sehwag or Tamim Iqbal coming in to bat and teeing off even in a Test match, but when Slats did it we were all amazed. He very quickly became a bar-emptying player and one that I think other professional cricketers would pay money to go and watch.

Being on the end of it was no fun as an England supporter, but you've got to take your hat off to him for staying true to his method and for being brave enough to face up to the opening bowlers and slap them around the park, knowing they would only bowl faster and shorter at him.

Since he has moved into the commentary box, Slats and I have got on like a house on fire and that is because what you see is what you get with him. The infectious enthusiasm you hear on TV is still there in the bar afterwards. He is a great guy who loves cricket and is one of the nicest blokes on the circuit. For someone who could be so vicious with a bat in his hand, he is actually very mild off the field.

He took England apart so many times that his departure from the Test side in 2001 came as blessed relief, but he should have played more. A player of his class and ability should have played at least 100 tests and he ended up 26 short of that number. He had dips in form, but he could tear teams apart with his style of batting. He, more than any other Australian cricketer, was the catalyst behind the increase in run rates from the late 1990s onwards, setting the standard to which Matthew Hayden then rose. Those are the sort of players that I love to watch, and standing at slip, I'd get a good view of some pretty entertaining cricket. If we didn't get him out early, we'd be in trouble, at least until he got to 90, then there would always be a chance. He would have had many more than his fourteen Test tons if he had converted some of his nine nineties into triple-figure scores.

SLATER V. ENGLAND

Played: 20
Won: 13
Drew: 3
Lost: 4
Runs: 1,669
Average: 45.10
Centuries: 7
Ashes won: 1993, 1994–95, 1998–99, 2001

THE COLONIAL
HEARTLAND

Winning the Ashes is a tremendous buzz full stop, but to win it away from home is something else; it is what I played cricket for. In 1978–79, I wanted to experience the full nine yards of an Ashes tour. I had been to Australia before, but only to Melbourne. This time, I was going to go to places that were barely even on the map and I couldn't wait.

I've always been an adventurous sort, so the chance to get out and see new places was a thrill for me and I wanted to soak it all up. I had been to Pakistan and New Zealand the previous winter and seen places that looked like they were ready to enter the '50s rather than the '80s, so I was excited about visiting Australia and also about bringing Kath out to see it with me. She could only come out for the start, because she was pregnant with Sarah, our second child. Initially, we had a bit of resistance from the TCCB when I made my formal request for Kath to join me. Those in charge really didn't like to see wives out with the players on tour and most definitely not at the start of a tour when everyone is bedding in, but, having already been away from Kath for long periods, I wasn't prepared to accept that.

Personally, I can understand that the beginning of a tour isn't the best time for the wives and girlfriends to come out, but they really should be encouraged to come out whenever possible beyond that. The players like having their partners around and it helps the touring party to become a much more normal group, and that is a good thing.

It is all very different these days, when the ECB (the England and Wales Cricket Board) actually pays for the wives and girlfriends to come out; that is one of the few things I think they should be applauded for. I know Kevin Pietersen is a big advocate of this and he now refuses to travel anywhere for too long without his wife, Jessica, and good on him for that.

In 1978, we had no choice about the timing of when Kath would come out, so once I had my polite letter rejected by Donald Carr and the TCCB committee, I had to argue my case a bit further. Again, the word came back that the answer was no. Enough was enough, as far as I was concerned, so I told Donald in no uncertain terms that if Kath didn't go, then I didn't go, and, surprise, surprise, they got back to me the following morning to say that they were very happy for her to come along.

So everything was now sorted and we were both really looking forward to getting out to Australia. I had only had a little taste of Ashes cricket at that stage and was desperate for more. The fact that since I had last been Down Under I had enjoyed some success against New Zealand and Pakistan meant that I would be going to Australia feeling more confident about my ability as a Test cricketer and, although I had still only played ten times for England, I knew that I would be in a good position to really give the Aussies what for.

With all my attention focused on the trip, I very nearly didn't make it at all after an unfortunate incident in a local pub. During some leaving drinks, I accidentally put my hand through a pane of glass. I was moving from one bar to another, somebody called me and, as I turned, I instinctively put my hand out to stop the swinging door from hitting me. It certainly wasn't like the incident that happened to Kiwi batsman Jesse Ryder, who put his hand through the toilet window in a bar after enjoying a few drinks, nor like the occasion when Mike Gatting returned to the Lord's pavilion and put his arm through the window of the door in anger at getting out. It was just one of those unlucky things. My wrist was cut and blood was pouring out of me like a fountain.

I went to hospital fearing the worst, but I was told not that my career was over but that I had been extremely fortunate to have severed two tendons and not the nerve. I think that might be the only time anyone's been happy to sever two tendons! As it was, it meant I would be out of commission for a few weeks, but I could go to Australia and I should certainly be fit enough for the first Test. Waiting for my injury to heal actually had a few plus points, if I'm honest. It meant that I could spend some decent time with Kath at the start of the trip without worrying too much about nets or training because I couldn't really do anything. And as far as I was concerned, no nets were good nets.

I missed out on the opening first-class match because of the injury and it turned out to be a good one to miss, as we lost to South Australia. When I returned for the game against New South Wales, I was straight back in amongst the action with a fifty and five wickets in the second innings as we got up and running with a ten-wicket win.

This was the sort of result expected of us and it really kick-started the tour. The side was under a fair bit of pressure to do well on this trip, unlike in recent years, when an Ashes tour has been a case of damage limitation.

We had the Ashes firmly tucked away following the 3–0 win in 1977, and due to World Series Cricket the Australian side were not expected to offer much resistance. We had lost a couple of players ourselves, but in truth the Aussies were likely to turn out a second-string side that we simply had to beat – and that was how it proved to be.

My second match of the tour was another loosener-up, in Queensland, out in the sticks against a group of local cricketers/farmers who would have loved to stick one on the Poms. It was up in Bundaberg, which is famous for its rum, but, trust me, there was nothing Caribbean about this place. It was pretty much in the middle of nowhere and could have come straight out of *The Flying Doctors*. Still, this was part and parcel of what made Ashes touring so special. You would go out to these small satellite places and have a game of cricket, get the mickey taken out of you all day and then have people – men and women – queuing up to drink you under the table afterwards. This was a typical such match, but I remember that game particularly due to one bloke called Scott Ledger.

Now, I've met some tough characters in my life, people who have gone through some pretty horrendous things and come out the other side, but when it comes to bravery and bloody-minded toughness, Scott Ledger is right up there. You will never have heard of him, but to me he sums up the fighting Aussie spirit and the competitive desire coursing through their veins when it comes to the Poms.

We were playing at Salter Oval in a 35-over match and we were batting first. It was a ground that was a little bit rough around the edges but it had been done up quite nicely for the day. However, there was no escaping the wire fencing that ran around part of the ground, and early on in our innings Scott chased after a boundary hit by Mike Brearley only to see the ball scoot under the fence. Nothing was going to stop this Crocodile Dundee from getting it back, but as he reached under the fence the wire sliced across his hand and there was claret everywhere. Seeing all that blood gushing from his hand as he ran back to the pavilion reminded me of what I had done just weeks earlier and I was worried for the poor bloke. He went off to the local hospital, which was probably about 500 miles away, got it all stitched up and then returned to the game ready to play again. None of us could quite believe it, but there he was, keen to stick it to us, and since he was their opening batsman, I can understand why he wanted his moment against the English.

I can't remember ever feeling too sorry for the Aussies when they got into a bit of bother against the quicks, but this time we didn't even have the satisfaction of having inflicted the damage ourselves. John Lever soon put that right, though.

Fully bandaged up, this guy went out to the middle to face our opening attack of JK and myself, and while I got into my stride, JK needed no second invitation to come tearing into him, give him a bouncer and clatter him straight on the head. There were hardly any helmets in those days, and certainly none out in the Aussie bush. Poor old Scott had to be helped from the field for the second time and he wasn't in a good way.

As the game wore on, imagine our surprise when he returned

to the field for a third go. He scurried through for a single or two, before JK gave him another bumper and lo and behold it smacked him on the head again. This time it really was all over as he hit the turf and saw more stars than there are on the Aussie flag. He had no choice but to retire hurt, but as he went off we all understood just how much it meant to the Australian public to have a go at the Poms – although we also thought 'look what happens if you try too hard!'

Anyway, we did have a great night there after the game and things were looking good for our side, led by our skipper Brearley. Brears really was a fine leader of men, with an ability to talk to anyone. He might have been seen as a bit of a toff, Oxbridge educated and all that, but he was better than that; he understood what each player needed to make them tick and he had no snobbery when it came to the dressing-room. He wanted a team of equals in which everybody was pulling in the same direction. How he got that was down to his ability; it was his greatest strength, and on that trip he was in his element.

With him and Kenny Barrington essentially in charge, I felt it was the ideal environment for me to succeed and, as an improving international cricketer, it was the perfect time to test myself in the harshest environment of them all.

Brisbane, though, became much harsher than I ever thought when the night before the Test Kath and I went to a local seafood restaurant and I devoured a plate of Oysters Kilpatrick. I now know why I've never met Patrick – those oysters must have killed him, as they nearly did me. I was as ill as I have ever been as a result of putting something in my mouth. Copious amounts of wine never seem to do me much harm, but on this occasion oysters and I fell out in a bad way. I'm happy to say that it hasn't stopped me from getting stuck in since. I know the old adage says that one bad oyster ruins it for you for ever, but each time I go back to Oz, New Zealand or especially South Africa, a plate of oysters is a must.

The night before the Test was pretty rough for me, though, and while Liam was busy making faces and noises in his cot, I was busy making far worse ones in the hotel bathroom as a result of those oysters.

The team physio, Bernard Thomas, and a local doctor came to my room and gave me a powerful sedative, which knocked me out after a while, but when Bernard tried to wake me the following morning, the task was not an easy one. Think grizzly bear in hibernation dreaming about catching fish by the river – you just wouldn't want to get up, would you? Eventually, he stirred me enough to get me up and out of bed by 10 a.m. and I made it to the ground just 20 minutes before the start of play.

I was glad that I did, though, because the time spent on the sidelines with my wrist and the long lead-up time to the first Test had me ready to burst by the time the game at the Gabba came around. I didn't care that this was effectively a scratch Aussie team due to defections to Packer. All I knew was that it was the Ashes and I had to do whatever I could to keep hold of them.

Looking back on this period, I readily accept that Australia were not as strong a side as they could have been, but what I will not accept is that it was easy to win. As Scott Ledger had proved early on in the tour, there is a strong fighting streak in the Aussie make-up and any chance they get to take on the Poms is a chance they will grab with both hands. There is simply no such thing as an Australian pushover. You could drag 11 guys off Bondi beach, stick them in whites and tell them the Ashes was at stake and you'd have to be at your best to beat them.

This Aussie team might have been stripped of the likes of the Chappells, Dennis Lillee and Rod Marsh, but they still had the exceptional Rodney Hogg with the ball and Kim Hughes with the bat, and midway through the series a certain Allan Border made his Ashes bow, so they weren't mugs by any stretch. It just takes a bit more than raw talent to create a successful Test side.

The opening day of the series set the tone, really, and thankfully, unlike in the 2006–07 series, when the first ball was pouched at second slip, this tone was a beautiful one to the ears of the England players and fans.

The Aussies won the toss and batted, and in the blink of an eye were 26–6 before limping to 116 all out in fewer than 40 overs. I had taken 3–40 and had pretty much sweated out the last remnants of that sedative-oyster mix, which allowed me to have a bit of a dart with the bat and score 49 as we enjoyed a 170-run lead on first innings.

Hogg was already amongst the wickets, though, with 6–74, and that was just a taste of what was to come from him during the series. Tons from Graham Yallop and Kim Hughes meant we had a target of 170 to chase down and we did it with ease to win by 7 wickets. Derek Randall had scored a pair of seventies in the game and looked in ominous touch.

Kath had to leave me before the next Test, and I was sorry to see her go because we'd enjoyed a nice time together away from all the pressures of home life and I think it was good for us. It also allowed her to see what touring life is like. While the boys will always want to enjoy themselves on tour, the reality is that some of the stories wildly exaggerate what actually happens, so it was good for Kath to see how normal things were.

After 12 Test matches of pretty much constant success, I was starting to consider that normal, but my 13th appearance turned out to be quite different as I had my worst personal performance for England so far.

A total of 41 runs and match figures of 0–100 highlight how difficult I found the game at Perth, but happily we had some pretty good players who did the business to secure the win anyway. David Gower built on his burgeoning reputation with a quality hundred before Bob Willis and John Lever did the damage with the ball and we won by 166 runs. Rodney Hogg picked up another ten wickets in the match, but Australia were proving to have a soft underbelly that we were happy to exploit.

As we moved on to Melbourne for the third Test it was my second successive Christmas away from home, and it was quite tough because Kath was heavily pregnant back in the UK. These days, the England cricket team will do anything to be at home for Christmas and the only tours they're away for are the Ashes and South Africa. I had five consecutive Christmases away, and that was simply the way it was.

Perhaps a few of the boys were feeling a little bit low at that time of year because we didn't cover ourselves in glory during the game, with Rodney Hogg once again our chief destroyer. His second ten-wicket haul in as many games did for us.

Although we only needed 283 to win, we were routed for 179 to lose by 103 runs.

It threw the series wide open and came as a complete shock to us all. But it served as the perfect reminder that there is no such thing as a weak Australian side.

Allan Border had begun his Test career with a win and Brears had suffered his first loss as England captain in 16 Test matches. Both of these men would have a huge impact on the Ashes in the years to come and, for me, they epitomised the best of captaincy in their respective countries.

Brears really came into his own after the defeat in Melbourne. It threatened to derail our mission to not just beat but totally dominate this Australian team. As a result, the skipper got us all together and issued a bit of a rallying cry. Usually, teams do this when they are down, but Brears knew that it was a make-or-break time in the trip, and he told us we had to start treating each day's play as if it were the very first of the series. The sense of expectation, enthusiasm and concentration that oozes out of every pore at the start of a series had to be with us each day from then on if we were to nip this Australian mini-revival in the bud. I think that he knew he was in a lose–lose position. If England won, it was only what was expected of him, but if we lost, it would have been his head on a platter. The best he could hope for was some satisfaction at a win.

We went into the New Year's Test in Sydney full of gusto, but it didn't work out that well for us to begin with. We were bowled out for just 152 with my own 59 top-scoring. By the close, they were 56–1 and cruising. In the end, to restrict them to 294 was a magnificent effort. Our second innings didn't start all that well either; Boycs going for a duck wasn't in his script, that's for sure.

But by the end of the third day, Arkle had begun a bit of a rescue operation and was 65 not out but with plenty of work to do. The next day, naturally, was a rest day, so a lot of the boys enjoyed a few drinks and then either had a day on the harbour or did something a bit cultural. My natural urge to go fishing was easily catered for in Sydney.

That evening, though, I suffered one of the two biggest problems that come with rooming with Arkle and from that day I vowed never to share another room with him. The first problem was his snoring, and with a schnozzer like his that is understandable. The second problem was his nervous, chatty, almost downright crazy disposition, which led to him keeping me up all night before we were due to play.

He had gone out exploring during the rest day and found himself a place to have a bite to eat. As he started walking back to the hotel, he realised that he was lost and couldn't even remember the name of the place we were staying. This went on for a few hours as he desperately tried to find out where he should be heading back to and he got himself in quite a state. When he eventually got back to the hotel, it was about three in the morning and he promptly walked into the room and woke me up to tell me what had happened before insisting that I have a cup of tea with him. Now, I don't mind staying up late, as long as there are a few drinks to go round, and I don't mean tea! By the time I finally managed to shut him up and get some sleep, it was six o'clock and I was shattered.

At the ground, I was fuming with him and told him he'd better not get out, so that I could get some kip in the changing-room. Good old Arkle, he did just as he was told and scored a remarkable 150 despite the night before. I only chipped in with eight, so as far as I was concerned we were never to be room-mates again!

His knock gave us something to bowl at, although it was only 205. There was a real chance of us ending the game all square, which would have been unthinkable. As it was John Emburey and Geoff Miller – our spin twins – took advantage of a turning, crumbling surface to bowl the Aussies out for 111 and secure the Ashes, which was a good thing, since Bob Willis had decided he didn't like the heat and could hardly bowl.

We went on to Adelaide feeling we'd escaped with a much-needed victory, and it gave us a bucketload of confidence to work with. Even though we were 27–5, I cracked 74 and shared a couple of partnerships with Miller and Emburey to put 169 on the board and then took 4–42 to give us an improbable 5-run lead. Second time around, Bob Taylor was our batting hero and deserved the hundred to go with it; alas, he fell three runs short and he never managed to get a ton after all. The target of 366 was far too much for the Aussies and a 205-run win meant a 4–1 scoreline going into the last.

All the talk was about how not since Douglas Jardine won the Ashes in the Bodyline series of 1932–33 had an England captain won four Tests on Australian soil, and now Brears was in the mood to be a record-breaker.

A 5–1 finish was just what he deserved and it would be so emphatic, a better result than people expected. He told us simply before the game, 'The series may be in the bag, but the job isn't done yet.'

We all took that to heart and I think our first innings summed up the desire of the whole team to perform. No one got a hundred, but nearly everyone made a contribution as we took a lead of 110, giving the spinners more than enough to play with back on their favourite ground, Sydney.

Our nine-wicket win meant a thrashing for Australia, and it felt good. Forget the strength of their side; we were given 11 men to play against each time and it was our job to beat them as best we could. I had scratched an itch that had been there since I'd started playing and I knew I wanted to keep on scratching.

The emergence of Border and the bowling of Hogg were just about the best things to come out of that series for the Aussies, and it wouldn't be long before they got their chance to play us again. But next time, unusually for a contest between the two sides, the Ashes was not at stake.

WHEN THE ASHES WASN'T THE ASHES

always find it curious to be told by some advert on TV or some billboard that an England team in a sport other than cricket and an Australian team in a sport other than cricket are playing each other for the Ashes. At first, I'm astonished that a group of hockey players or rugby players or lawn-green bowls players are suddenly going to down their jacks or whatever and start playing cricket well enough to merit selection. Then I realise that they are going to be playing their own game, but the 'Ashes' are up for grabs. Well, they most certainly are not. The only time the Ashes are at stake is when England's cricketers meet Australia's cricketers over a series of five or more Tests.

The fact is that everyone wants to be associated with the Ashes. It is the oldest competition of its kind, and the history, tradition and stature it has developed over more than a hundred years are what people want to be a part of. I don't blame them, because it is so special. But back off – the Ashes is not for everybody to have a dart at.

With that in mind, it was a very strange feeling to be a part of an England side that went to Australia to play Test cricket against the national team but without the Ashes at stake.

In 1979, we headed Down Under for a three Test series against the old enemy as part of a brave new world of cricket thanks to Kerry Packer. His coup had worked, the Australian Cricket Board were happy to let him televise the matches on his Channel 9 network and he wanted a big summer's cricket to fill his schedules. What better than an Ashes contest?

But at such short notice, he wanted to crowbar a West Indies tour into the proceedings too. With Australia playing piecemeal Test cricket against both sides, there was also the matter of a triangular World Series Cup between all three teams, which was shoehorned in between the Test matches. In truth, it was a mess and I can't say I enjoyed it.

As far as I'm concerned, any time England play Australia it should be a serious business and the Ashes should be up for grabs. That means at least five Tests as the main event of either their or our summer. Nothing else will do – otherwise you begin to cheapen and tarnish what makes the contest so very special.

Packer, though, wanted his big-money series and he got it. No doubt there was a considerable bit of cash flying in the direction of both governing bodies for the privilege. It was the start of television money paving the way for the game's future. The big-money deals we see today between Sky Sports and the ECB or ESPN and the Indian Premier League are just following in Packer's footsteps, and they are a blessing for the game as long as the TV companies work side by side with the administrators in the best interests of the game.

In so many ways, this winter trip to Australia was the rebirth of international cricket as we know it now. The innovations of World Series Cricket, such as floodlit matches and coloured clothing, would become par for the course, while the split international schedule, with the Windies touring alongside us, was to become a feature all around the world. The days of one touring side hitting the shores of either England or Australia for a summer are long gone and it all started in 1979–80. I can remember back then it got a bit of a thumbs down from the England management and I could understand that because it was quite a disjointed tour. We had Test cricket followed by one-day cricket followed by Test cricket and there was very little flow to the tour. These days, tours have one-day sections and Test sections, which make them a lot easier to manage, especially when there are separate squads chosen for each format. That wasn't quite the case in my day. Everyone played everything and it took a bit of time for people to work out that one-day cricket had a style all of its own.

As far as we were concerned, though, our biggest challenge of that winter was the three Test matches against Australia, who had all their Packer players available again. Dennis Lillee and Jeff Thomson would naturally be opening the bowling. Teaming up with Rodney Hogg, they would be a handful without question. In the batting, Greg Chappell was back to lead and craft an innings alongside that little gem they'd found called Allan Border.

We started in Perth at the WACA, which was as quick and bouncy a pitch as you were likely to find in the world. And, as a bona fide Western Australian, Dennis Lillee couldn't wait to get stuck in, although as it turned out the thing he got stuck into most was the umpires and the two captains for not letting him use his aluminium bat.

Now Dennis is one of the game's greatest-ever bowlers, but a batsman he certainly isn't. I could understand his theory that he wanted any advantage he could get when it came to walking to the crease, but this piece of metal he carried out with him was just a joke and, to be honest, I couldn't see why he got so upset when he was told he couldn't use it. I mean, it's not as though he would have laid the bat on the ball anyway!

There was a curious stand-off, with DK having to be persuaded by Chappell to use a proper bat, and in his anger he hurled this metal object across the turf, which got the crowd going. I've spoken to Dennis about that episode since and he claims that his actions were born of frustration, that he'd felt that despite the new world order as a result of Kerry Packer, the game's authorities were still against any real innovation. Dennis had been banging his head against a brick wall for years as a player and having finally got his pay day with Packer and managed to effect change in Australia, he thought the metal bat wouldn't be a problem. When it was, all his frustrations of years gone by came pouring out and that is why he threw it. He can look back on it now and laugh because it is part of cricketing folklore, but it was no laughing matter back then. Ironically, DK went on to be the main man in charge of the MRF Pace Bowling Academy in India, the Madras Rubber Factory being the biggest supplier of wooden cricket bats in the world!

We knew we were up against it on this trip. We'd been getting quite a bit of stick from the Aussie fans and there was definitely a change in attitude towards us. It has never been sweetness and light out in Australia, but the banter always used to flow back to being good-natured. This time, however, there was definitely an edge that I hadn't noticed a year earlier.

It didn't really bother me, because the opinions of idiots in the crowd have never been anything other than the opinions of idiots and I've generally got better things to think about than that. But it didn't make it any easier for most of the squad. Brears came in for some real aggro on that trip because of what he'd done last time, winning five matches in their back yard. Yet he remained pretty calm about it all; behind his studious looks, there was a rod of steel running through him and it would take more than a few choice words to throw him off his guard. Brears was sporting a full bushy beard for the tour and had been nicknamed 'the Ayatollah' after the Iranian leader Ayatollah Khomeini.

After winning the toss in Perth, he asked Australia to bat and we started reasonably enough, dismissing them for 244 with a useful contribution of 6–78 from me in 35 overs of hard yakka.

We didn't bat so well, though. Derek Randall and Geoff Boycott both got ducks, so things weren't looking up, until Brears dug in and made a valuable 64, and, on his debut, a man who was to become a batting thorn in Australia's side, Graham Dilley, showed a glimpse of what he could do with a hard-earned 38 not out. The lead was just 16, so we had a more than sporting chance of getting a win if we could skittle them second time around. Unfortunately, that little leftie Border wouldn't budge and despite me grabbing another five-fer he took all the plaudits with 115 to set us 357 to win. Most likely, though, was a draw, if we could see out the end of the fourth and the fifth day. Boycs set about doing just that and was at his most cussed in a knock of 99, but there just wasn't enough support for him and we lost by 138 runs.

There was a funny moment, though, from that first defeat, when Border eventually got out and stormed back to the dressing-room in a right old huff. He was swearing and cursing as he hurled his bat across the room, giving the Poms what for as his rage bubbled over. It was only when he had calmed down a touch that he looked up and realised that in all the confusion he had marched straight into the England dressing-room and had aimed his abuse of the Poms straight at England tour manager and chairman of selectors Alec Bedser!

On to Sydney and a real seamer's paradise. There had been a lot of rain around before the game, thanks to an incredible thunderstorm over New Year's. The only problem was that the groundstaff had been given some time off to enjoy themselves, so the pitch had been left uncovered and suffered the consequences. It meant the pitch was a bit patchy and was likely to do all sorts, so whoever won the toss would bowl first and have plenty of fun. It wasn't us.

Before we even had the toss, there was an incident that sticks out in my mind because it was the first time I ever saw the normally calm and mild-mannered Brears lose his cool. Boycs had woken up on the morning of the match with a stiff neck and told Brears that he didn't think he could play. With things not going too well, the last thing Brears needed was to have his most experienced and reliable opener sit this one out, so he suggested he go and try it out in the indoor nets to see how it would affect him. Cleverly, Brears also sent a couple of others to watch him and see how he went. They came back and reported that he looked a little awkward but could bat reasonably well. That made Brears' mind up for him. Boycs would be playing and that was that. When Boycs then came to him and told him that it was no good and he couldn't play, they had a bit of a row.

There was just no way that Brears was going to let him off the hook. With Lillee, Geoff Dymock and Len Pascoe straining at the leash, he wanted his best opener to go out and face the music, stiff neck or not. In many ways, it was a compliment to Boycs, but he didn't quite see it that way and got upset, while a determined Brears wouldn't budge. It was rare to see the skipper lose it, but Boycs managed to make it happen, until he agreed to get on with it and play.

Thankfully, there was no Thommo to deal with in that game, but Lillee and Dymock more than made up for his absence as the ball moved this way and that until we were routed for 123. The only good thing about that was that it gave us a chance to have a go right back, and I grabbed another four wickets to continue my good form with the ball as we got them out for 145.

David Gower almost saved the series for us thereafter with a lovely 98 not out before he ran out of partners. It was an important innings for 'Lubo' (the nickname comes from his favourite restaurant in Adelaide) because he showed everyone that he really did have the class of a genius when it came to batting, and he would go from strength to strength.

Australia, though, chased their target of 216 to win by six wickets and the series was gone. In the dressing-room afterwards, there was a slightly strange feeling to it all. We were obviously upset to have lost, but the fact that whoever won the toss in Sydney was bound to win made us feel a little resigned to that result – plus the fact that the Ashes weren't at stake also made the hurt a bit easier to bear. There just wasn't the same feel to it at all.

That is why something like that must never be allowed to happen again. The Ashes is too important for gimmicks like this. The fact that we were professional cricketers and knew no other way of playing a Test match than at full tilt shouldn't cover up the fact that having the Ashes on the line is what makes these matches so special. It is also part of the reason why I want to see the Ashes stored in whichever country holds them, but more on that later.

When we got to Melbourne, I think we were all in the mood for some revenge, to show that we were better than the scoreline suggested, and things got off to a decent enough start, with a century opening stand for the first time on the trip. However, Australia cruised past our total of 306, thanks to a Greg Chappell ton, to put us up against it.

Lillee was in great form yet again and really showed what a

clever bowler he was by reducing his speed to bowl dangerous cutters that did for most of our batsmen. I finally managed to cut loose and show the Aussies why people were calling me an all-rounder and not just a bowler as I made my first-ever Test hundred against them. It had been a while coming, with it being my 11th match against them, but it was a very satisfying feeling. I would go on to get three more hundreds against the Aussies and each time I knew that to get to three figures against them was a real achievement. They don't just give them away. Still, personal milestones mean very little against a backdrop of defeat, and an eight-wicket loss represented a miserable tour for us, despite my own personal success.

I left that tour telling myself two things. First, that the Australians were back and they would never again be the pushovers they had been in 1978–79. When the Ashes would be up for grabs in 1981, it would be a serious affair that would settle the dispute over who was better in this era once and for all. Second, I knew that I was now in my prime as an international cricketer and I could not afford to waste it. I've always been impetuous and felt like I needed to be at the centre of everything, but sometimes it is difficult to back up those thoughts with deeds and ability. After this trip, I was in no doubt that I not only belonged in international cricket but could do some serious damage. I was still young, fit and strong, but with enough experience behind me to know exactly what I was doing. I knew how to get people out, and I knew how to construct a proper Test match innings. I just felt like it was my time and if something needed doing on the field, then I was the man to do it.

We went to India after that series to play the Golden Jubilee Test in Bombay and it is fair to say that I went hell for leather, on and off the field, and it worked. I bowled and bowled, I batted, I worked hard for the team and let's just say I enjoyed myself off the pitch too.

As a commentator now, I wonder whether the balance is right. The England team trains harder than it has ever done before and they have an army of physios and fitness gurus telling them to jump on top of tractor tyres or get in the gym and lift big weights, yet when it comes to getting on with the job in hand and the business of bowling or batting, I'm not sure how much difference it makes.

I bring this up now because I have been there and done it and during this period in 1979–80 I was as strong and as fit as I have ever been, and I got that way by playing cricket and bowling overs. I bowled 40 overs in the first innings at Melbourne and then went out and scored a hundred with the bat. I left Australia and went to India, where I hit a hundred in Bombay and then bowled 26 overs on the reel because that was my job and I knew how to do it. Nothing has angered me more in recent years than the opening exchanges of the 2006–07 Ashes tour when our 'fit' players went there undercooked and unready for Test match cricket. They might have been able to hit 14 on the bleep test, but that's not what gets Ricky Ponting out – bowling does.

My personal success in Australia and India came alongside an elevation to the players' management committee on tour. Clearly, Brears saw something in me that he thought would be worthwhile sharing with the rest of the group. More likely, it was that he probably thought I would get into less trouble if I had a bit of responsibility on my shoulders. I'm not sure that was strictly true, but I was happy enough to go along with it.

However, when we got back from the trip, it was clear that Brears was ready to hand over the reins. He knew he didn't want to tour again the following winter, as he was looking to concentrate on his career as a psychoanalyst. While I hadn't really considered myself captaincy material before this point, the fact that people were talking about me possibly taking on the job had me thinking. Everything else I had turned my hand to on a cricket field had paid off, so why not this? I understood the game and I knew what was required to win matches, so surely that was enough to skipper the side. And if it wasn't, then I was sure I could pull a performance out of the bag in any case.

Things such as man-management weren't really a part of the Ian Botham guide to captaincy and perhaps that was why things didn't work out so well. However, from the outset I was determined to give it my best shot, and I wasn't going to let anything stop me from taking a job that I knew I would love.

My first Test as a captain was against the unstoppable West Indies machine of the era and it is safe to say I had little to no chance of ending the dominance of King Viv and his boys, although I certainly tried. To be fair, the 1–0 loss that summer wasn't the worst effort on our part against such a magnificent team, but I already felt under pressure as captain and my first serious injury was hampering me beyond all measure.

At the start of the season, I had been playing in a county match against Oxford University at the Parks and felt a twinge in my back for the first time, possibly as a result of not warming up properly. It had gradually got worse throughout the summer, so that by the end I was in almost constant agony.

With the Windies tour of 1980 out of the way, we were welcoming the Aussies to our shores for a celebratory Centenary Test fully one hundred years after the first match between our two countries had been played in England. Although the first one had been played at the Oval, this rematch was at Lord's and although the match itself, ruined by rain and ending in a draw, wasn't a classic, it was certainly a memorable one for me.

The rain had completely taken the second day out of commission and a section of the third day too, so as captain I was part of the discussions with the umpires as to when the game might be restarted. Dickie Bird was quite concerned about the state of the ground and didn't think we should be playing, and I agreed with him. The MCC members, though, had come to see some cricket and were less than impressed with the decision to delay play until 3.45 p.m.

After one of our inspections, a few of the members made their feelings known, not just with the usual barracking but also with a bit of argy-bargy, and they went for umpire David Constant. Now, that just wasn't on, so together with Greg Chappell I actually stepped in to stop a fight, rather than, as in years gone by, jumping in to start one!

Australia were definitely in a better position, as they were working their way towards 385–5 declared, and looking back on it now perhaps I should have been a bit more understanding about the need to play cricket to keep the fans happy. But when you are in that situation, you just don't want to give the Aussies anything.

I'm often frustrated these days when the game shoots itself in the foot and denies paying spectators the chance to watch their heroes, a classic example being the Twenty20 international at Old Trafford that was cancelled in 2009 due to a small damp patch near the wicket. It is not good enough. Unlike in my day, when the status quo could rumble along without too much of a worry because there were limits on what people could do with their time, right now cricket is competing in an overcrowded marketplace and cannot continue to let fans down. At least in 1980 it was just a bit of jostling, which Greg and I could handle.

In the end, Greg tried to set up a bit of a run chase, and although Geoff Boycott and Mike Gatting both batted well for a hundred and a fifty respectively, we couldn't really force the pace for the win and it was honours even.

What it did mean was that I would be more than up for the task of taking on the Aussies as captain in a full Ashes series the following summer – as long as things went smoothly enough in the Caribbean.

FANTASY TEAM 2

MIDDLE ORDER

MICHAEL VAUGHAN (C)

Vaughany will always be remembered as the man who finally brought the Ashes back and, for that incredible summer of 2005, I have no hesitation in making him my captain. But he would get into this team anyway, because as a batsman against Australia he was awesome. He was a tremendous player in general but, out of all the countries he played against, I think he shone the most against the Aussies. They brought out the best in 'Virgil'.

I've got to know him a bit better since he retired from the game, having spent a few hours on the golf course with him in recent months, and there is an awful lot to Michael Vaughan that people don't really get to see.

We went up to play some golf at Archerfield Links not too long ago and we stayed in a lodge together, having a few glasses of red wine late into the evenings, which taught me a bit more about him than I'd previously known, like his average – but improving – taste in wine. For a start, he won't let you off the hook if you've made a bet and lost on the golf course. He is extremely competitive and won't give you a chance if he gets his nose in front, and that is how it should be. He admitted that there was no room for second-guessing yourself as a captain in an Ashes series. He said there is always a temptation to change things around if things aren't going well, but sometimes it is not a change of plan that is required, just the belief to know that what you have will work for you. And that is why he was so successful in 2005. He kept calm and kept the faith in his side when others quickly deserted following the defeat at Lord's, and that is what you need from your captain: calm assurance that rubs off on the other players.

He is a thinker, which was a huge part of his ability as a captain, but he is also an extremely tough character with an inner steel and I really like that about him. You cannot dream of doing well against Australia if you've not got a hard edge somewhere, a part of you that relishes the fight, and Vaughan had that as a batsman and as a man. His performances in the 2002–03 series were nothing short of miraculous when you consider that his teammates gave him so little support. To go to Australia and score three hundreds in a series is career-defining and the fact that Vaughany was briefly recognised as the world's best batsman in an era when Tendulkar, Lara and Ponting were at their peak speaks volumes for him.

You would simply back Vaughan to score runs at number three for you in an Ashes battle, and although he hardly needs it, what gives him the edge over other batsmen is the way he scores his runs. He is one of the most stylish and pleasing to watch batsmen the English game has ever produced. I could watch Vaughan bat all day and not be bored, and considering I get bored waiting for him to putt, that is a fair old compliment. His record stands up to scrutiny alongside the very best, but we mustn't forget just how hard he had to fight with his degenerative knee condition, which robbed him of at least another 20 Test matches and the 2006–07 Ashes campaign. I can't say that England wouldn't have lost had he been fit and available, but I'm certain the scoreline would not have been 5–0, and I know that irks him as much as it does me to this day.

Vaughan v. Australia

Played: 10
Won: 3
Drew: 2
Lost: 5
Runs: 959

Average: 47.95
Centuries: 4
Ashes won: 2005

KEVIN PIETERSEN

KP has the potential to be England's greatest batsman, full stop. Goochie didn't make this list, unfortunately, but he still stands atop the run-scoring chart. I wonder for how much longer.

Kevin has been to Australia once already and did OK personally, but was stung by the team's performance. He took the 5–0 drubbing very badly indeed, and although there is a lot of bravado and confidence about him, there is no question he has thought long and hard about how he will be a part of a team that can get their own back. I can see him heading Down Under in 2010 and achieving something similar to what Michael Vaughan and Chris Broad did before him.

He is now back to his best following his Achilles injury and the time he spent out of the game, not to mention the palaver over the captaincy, which was so shoddily handled by the ECB. All in all, it cost him a year of his international career, but barring any mishaps from here on in, he could produce something magical in Australia, not just once but maybe twice. A star was born in 2005 and at the Oval he gave us a glimpse of what he could do on the biggest stage of all, but I believe he is better than that now.

I know KP pretty well and he is not one of life's bit-part players. He wants to be out front and leading the way, so even though he played in a couple of the Ashes matches in 2009, he didn't really get involved in the way he wanted to. That was why he just hung back a little in the celebrations at the Oval, unlike four years previously, and although he was delighted that the team won, he is desperate for a starring role. There is nothing wrong with that at all; every team needs its generals and lieutenants, and when Pietersen is firing, so too are England.

He also understands what Ashes cricket is about. He knows what it means for England to win and the passion burns brightly in him. Forget all the chat about being South African and whatever, he is a proud Englishman when he walks onto the field. He understands the responsibility that comes with being an England player in the Ashes and he loves it. You can't teach someone that.

He can also get under the skin of the Australians. They don't like playing him because he gives as good as he gets and he doesn't bend to their will. He has their respect, but they want to see the back of him more than any other England player right now, and it would be a real treat to see how someone like AB would deal with KP.

PIETERSEN V. AUSTRALIA

Played: 12
Won: 3
Drew: 3
Lost: 6
Runs: 1,116
Average: 50.72
Centuries: 2
Ashes won: 2005, 2009

DAVID GOWER

David will always walk into any fantasy team of mine because he was simply the finest English batsman I ever played with. I say English because Viv was the very best, in my opinion, but Lubo wasn't too far behind.

When he strolled to the crease to bat, you stopped what you were doing and paid attention. You watched not just because he was elegance personified or because if he was in the mood he could take a bowling attack apart quite viciously but because you wanted to try to work out how he managed to have so much time to play the shots he did, how he managed to make batting look so easy when he had the likes of Thommo steaming in at him. That was the skill that set him apart from the rest.

He is a great friend of mine and 99 times out of 100 is a pleasure to be around. He is one of the most laid-back men you are ever likely to meet, with the exception of Chris Gayle, but watch out when that fuse does go, because it is volcanic.

I used to enjoy playing cricket with Lubo and especially batting with him, because we could discuss all sorts out in the middle, usually what type of wine we might tuck into that evening. Lubo was also much more interested in how the opposition were reacting to us than the other way round. Back in 1986 in Brisbane, we had a right old time of it smashing the ball to all parts as I got a hundred and he got a fifty. He tried to rein me in at times because he was convinced I'd get out to one of my big shots, but he soon realised that he was wasting his time, and as the Aussies grew more frustrated we just kept on enjoying ourselves. There was nothing he loved more than to see the opposition bowlers' shoulders slumping, because he knew we were on top then. He was a great reader of body language and I think that is part of the reason he was able to fool a lot of people with his own. People thought he didn't care because he looked so relaxed, but he did, passionately.

When the Aussies were the opponents, he steeled himself for battle, and the way he played in 1985 was as ruthless as anyone could have been. I think to be a top-class batsman you have to be a bit selfish, you have to want the strike and want to score runs and want to have the adulation that comes from that, and Lubo was no different. Even though Boycs, KP and Lubo are all wildly different characters, they all have that trait running through them and that is why they've achieved the things they have.

Gower and Australia are natural bedfellows both on and off the field, and in any side you need to have men who are going to be fun to be around. Obviously to make this fantasy series fair we would have to play at home and away, and Lubo is a cracking tourist as his little escapade in the Tiger Moth showed – there wouldn't be any recriminations for jinks like that in my team!

GOWER V. AUSTRALIA

Played: 42
Won: 14
Drew: 12
Lost: 16
Runs: 3,269
Average: 44.78
Centuries: 9
Ashes won: 1978–79, 1981, 1985, 1986–87

RICKY PONTING

Is there a tougher cricketer than Ricky Ponting playing the game? I doubt it.

He is uncompromising in the way that Steve Waugh was before him, but with a much bigger range of strokes to beat you with. He is a man I'd want in the trenches with me because he never shirks from anything on or off the field.

As a youngster, he had his run-ins with authority and was a bit of a wild thing, but with a bit of age and experience on his side he has matured into one of the greatest players the game has ever known. There can be no doubt whatsoever about his ability – his record is there – and the fact that he has led his country the number of times he has and gained the respect he has around the world proves that he is a giant of the game.

With more self-belief than even Geoff Boycott, Ponting is up in the highest bracket of Test cricket. For me, he is in the top five of all time. I never saw Don Bradman play cricket, but the very best I've seen include Viv Richards, Brian Lara, Sachin Tendulkar, David Gower and Ricky Ponting. He is a supreme batsman who has managed to scale heights that other great players can only dream of. During one incredible run in 2002, which included the Ashes campaign at the end of the year, he scored eight Test tons in thirteen matches, which is just mind-boggling. You thought here was an exceptional player in a zone that many never get into; if you're lucky, you might get to that place once in your career.

Ponting already had my admiration for that, but then in 2005 and 2006 he went and scored ten tons in another thirteen matches, including the most miserable Ashes series of the lot. That told me a few things about Ponting, which were that he is better than good when it came to batting, also that he peaks for the contests that matter most to him – which have long been and will always be the Ashes – and finally that his desire to do well doesn't stem from personal success – because you get bored of that pretty quickly – it comes from his team's success, and he never gets bored of that.

He was a vital piece in the Australian machine that won 16 Test matches in a row under Steve Waugh in 1999–2000, but then he led his own team to the same streak in 2005–07, and you cannot argue with a record and a desire to win like that.

There are some out there who pick holes in his tactics at times and believe that he should have won more matches than he has done, but that is utter rubbish. He has done the very best with the tools he has had at his disposal, which have been pretty impressive. His greatest achievement as a captain might not be all the success he had with Warne and McGrath, but the wins he got without them. I know that he still hurts from having lost the Ashes on English soil twice, but he can revel in the satisfaction of masterminding a 5–0 drubbing at home too. When Ponting retires, there will be a couple of holes in his cricketing CV because of 2005 and 2009, but not even a third defeat at home could eclipse the fact that if you needed a man to score you a hundred in any circumstance whatsoever, you would ask Ricky to do it. He picked up his first against England in 1997, when there were some who doubted whether he would make the most of his ability, and by the time he hit 150 in Cardiff he had raised his bat 38 times. No Ashes cricketer comes close to that bar the Don.

PONTING V. ENGLAND

    Played: 31
    Won: 19
    Drew: 5
    Lost: 7
    Runs: 2,363
    Average: 48.22
    Centuries: 8
    Ashes won: 1997, 1998–99, 2001, 2002–03, 2006–07

GREG CHAPPELL

One of the most talented batsmen I have ever had the misfortune of playing against. There is no question that he was the most naturally gifted of the three Chappell siblings to play for Australia, and he was a gentleman with it. I first watched him play when he was Somerset's overseas player in the late 1960s. I only saw him a couple of times, but he had an impact on me as a bloke who could bat beautifully and also bowl useful medium pace. He was a supremely gifted batsman and a genuine all-rounder.

He was so stylish in the way he played that you couldn't help but want to play like him. In later years, when we played against each other I would often stand at slip marvelling at some of his effortless shots and have a dig at Boycs, asking him, 'Why don't you play like that?' He'd then get out and Boycs would say, 'That's why. Because you can't get many runs in the pavilion!'

As a side, we always put a big prize on Greg Chappell's wicket because we knew he could rip us apart in much the same way Gower could when he had got in. You never wanted Greg to get in because there was a fair old chance he'd go on and make a hundred. But when he did get in and was in the mood, he could play the sort of innings that would have you almost applauding his shots even though you were trying to get him out. We had Gower and they had Chappell, and the comparison is a good one because they were the players who brought a touch of finesse to each side. They would be the classiest batsmen on show in this fantasy game.

Greg was like a surgeon, so precise and accurate in what he was doing, and he never seemed to get flustered or caught up in the excitement. He kept a very even keel. Only once did I see him get a bit tetchy and that was when we were opposing captains in the 1980 Centenary Test at Lord's and the crowd got a bit restless at the lack of cricket due to the poor weather. Some of them jostled the umpires, causing me and Greg to get involved. He didn't shirk from getting stuck in to keep the peace there, which was the right thing to do, but afterwards, I remember, he wasn't very impressed with it all and was keen to point out the guilty party to the MCC.

He was also his own man, which is a bit of a theme running through both of my fantasy elevens. He was one of the most high-profile movers to World Series Cricket and I think cricketers of our and subsequent generations have an awful lot for which to thank those who played. For the record, he was one of the stand-out performers in WSC against a full-strength West Indies side that took no prisoners.

But it was in the Ashes that he enjoyed his finest hour.

Having made himself unavailable for the 1981 tour for personal reasons, he returned to face us in 1982–83, and although he was coming towards the end of his career, he was incredible. A ton in Perth and another in Adelaide helped confirm the Aussies' superiority on that trip and gave them back the Ashes before he retired.

CHAPPELL V. ENGLAND

Played: 35
Won: 13
Drew: 13
Lost: 9
Runs: 2,619
Average: 45.94
Centuries: 9
Ashes won: 1974–75, 1975, 1982–83

ALLAN BORDER (C)

If there was a man to credit with Australia's dominance over the past 15 years, it wouldn't be Ricky Ponting or Steve Waugh, nor even Shane Warne or Glenn McGrath, although they all played a role. Allan Border is the man to revere and thank or despise and moan at depending on your allegiance. He is the man who changed Australian cricket and put them on the road to total domination.

There is no question that they would not have had the success they've had without the unbelievable players at their disposal, but Border turned them from a rabble into a team that was hard to beat, and by the time he retired they were the best side in the world. He saw it all and carved out his own place in cricket history.

He led Australia out of the dark and that is why he is the captain of my fantasy side, because he was the ultimate leader of men. He might not have been the most naturally charismatic bloke, or a genius tactician, but he was tough, uncompromising and thoughtful. Put that together with fantastic ability with the bat and you have one hell of a captain.

His batting was a lesson in consistency and playing the game in the way that suited you best. He didn't have the full range of strokes that a Ponting or Tendulkar has; instead, he made the absolute most of his strengths and succeeded more often than not. He would get into any world side of mine for his batting alone, but it is the way he dragged his team up after the Packer affair that really makes him stand out. Australian cricket was in the doldrums and he was a pretty friendly sort of cricketer, but he quickly realised that being friendly didn't win cricket matches and that was all he wanted to do . . . win.

We have been good friends regardless for a long time, although that was put aside during the Ashes series of 1989, when, he told me, 'I was prepared to be as ruthless as I had to be to stuff you.' And that he was.

He had an inner strength and steel to him and did not suffer fools at all. If he thought someone wasn't pulling his weight, he would let him know about it. I knew all about it at times, having played under him for Queensland and been the victim of one or two explosions. I think Craig McDermott got off lightly in 1993 when AB called him over from fine leg to have a word and he gave him some back-chat. 'I'm f***ing talking to you,' said AB as McDermott sulked back to his mark. 'Do that again and you're on the next plane home . . . You f***ing test me again and you'll see.' He was a man on a mission. He wanted Australia to be the best. When he gave up the mantle, it was carried on with relish by the next generation, but their success started with him.

I can't thank AB enough for the support he has given me over the years with my charity work, and he's even taken up doing charity walks back in Oz after I told him I had never seen an Aussie walk in my life!

I never liked it when he beat me and vice versa, but we respected each other and enjoyed some great battles. A better illustration than anything I can say of what Allan Border means to Australian cricket and Ashes cricket is the fact that the country's player of the year award is called the Allan Border Medal and the ceremony is the gala night of the year. It is only what he deserves.

BORDER v. ENGLAND

Played: 47
Won: 20
Drew: 15
Lost: 12
Runs: 3,548
Average: 56.31
Centuries: 8
Ashes won: 1982–83, 1989, 1990–91, 1993, 1994–95

THE GREATEST SERIES

It was midsummer in Leeds and we were playing the Australians at Headingley, but every time I bowled a ball it came out of my hand slower than the last time. No matter how fast I ran in or how much effort I put into delivering that ball, it would just come floating out of my hand and the batsman would launch it straight back over my head for six. I got angry, ran in even harder, but nothing changed . . . then I woke up.

It was still spring, the 1981 cricket season was almost upon us and I was having bad dreams about facing the Australians.

That has been the only time in my life when I've worried about playing Australia – when I've been sleeping! I laughed it off at the time, not really thinking much of it, since it was only a dream, but I can see now that it highlighted just what sort of turmoil I was in having lost the previous series in the Caribbean as well as losing a mentor in the shape of Ken Barrington. My record as captain hadn't been great. I thought there were mitigating circumstances, but people were already calling for my head. No wonder I wasn't sleeping well.

Still, when Alec Bedser called me to ask whether I would captain the side in the Texaco Trophy one-day series, I jumped at the chance and relaxed a little. I was really looking forward to the contest and felt it would give my era of captaincy the boost it needed for me to go on and do the job for a long time – few hopes can have been more emphatically dashed than that one was.

Still, I looked up and down the Australian team sheet and fancied my team would not only win the three-match one-day series but keep hold of the Ashes we had won so convincingly in 1978–79, even though all the Packer players were back in the fold. It didn't quite work out that way.

We lost the one-day series narrowly, 2–1, with the second game going right down to the wire before the Aussies won by two runs, which prompted the Australian journos to give their skipper, Kim Hughes, an ovation when he walked into the post-match press conference, something I certainly never received in my career (although you've probably got to win a game to get that!).

I had been confident before the series, but not overly so, suggesting that Australia could still be a handful on their day, but for some reason that was forgotten in the aftermath of defeat and once again my neck was on the line, with people questioning whether or not I should lead the side into the Ashes.

I was in no doubt that I should do it, so when I got pulled to one side by Alec Bedser during the third one-dayer to be asked to do the job in the Ashes, I was delighted, until he said they were giving me the role for one match only. That situation was far from ideal to my mind, but of course I accepted it straight away. Anything else would have been a sign of uncertainty or lack of confidence, and that wasn't me.

I look back on that little period now and although we now know what subsequently happened, I don't think my opinion has softened on this one. A captain is the captain of the side until either he is sacked or he resigns. Appointing a bloke on a match-by-match basis in cricket is just ludicrous for so many reasons and that is why it is never done like that any more, thank goodness. Alec went on to say to the press, 'We are only doing what Australia have done for years in home series. It may bring extra pressure on Ian, but playing Test match cricket is all about pressure.' I was angered by this comment because copying another country for the sake of it makes no sense. Why should we have to copy Australian cricket? We're not Australian! There are some aspects of sport and life where you take the best bits that you've learned from others and put them to good use, but you have to have solid foundations for doing so. What I never got from the selectors was why they wanted to copy the Australian system. I suspected that it just gave them an easy get-out clause if they wanted to sack me. So in one fell swoop, any idea I had that the selectors had confidence in me was gone.

Without getting too philosophical about it, what does it say about people when they are clearly looking for a way to make sure the crap doesn't stick to them when things go wrong rather than being keen to get their hands dirty in helping you out of a tough situation? Quite simply, the selectors had lost faith in me and I in them, but for the good of the England team we would muddle along for the time being.

I tried valiantly to tell myself that I was still the England captain, that I was still the best man to lead the side and that everybody else wanted me to, but it was hopeless. I knew from the off that I had to win to save my job and that brought with it all sorts of pressures that I wasn't really used to.

The thing was that up until then my career had been a bit of a breeze. I had done well in good sides and won a few games along the way. By that point, I had enough of a reputation for people to turn up and watch me play expecting something special, and on a fair number occasions I was able to provide that. Once I became England captain, life wasn't such a smooth ride and that can be reasonably hard to deal with at 25 years old when you think you know everything but don't. I was married with a couple of kids and life had generally been good to me until now. Previously, when there had been the odd blip, I could rely on bluster and bravado to get me through; now I no longer could, and nor could I rely on my ability to play cricket, because my form had deserted me. I had already gone 15 innings without a score higher than 37 by the time the opening Trent Bridge Test came along, and it was 18 innings of bowling since I had got my last five-fer, which was unusual for me.

To this day, I maintain that I was right to soldier on and try to claim the Ashes back as England captain, and perhaps I needed to go through the pain I was about to in order for the incredible things to happen that subsequently did. But objectively it was clear to see that I was on a hiding to nothing.

Kim Hughes won the toss and, under heavy skies, put us in to bat. It is exactly what I would have done myself. Dennis Lillee ripped through our top order with a masterful spell of quick swing bowling. DK had not long been released from hospital after suffering a pretty serious chest infection, but he showed no ill effects that day. He couldn't really bowl the long spells as a result of it, so he simply made them short and just as effective. While he took care of the top order, Terry Alderman and Rodney Hogg looked after the middle and lower orders. Rodney was a fine bowler but never quite hit the same heights as he did in his debut Ashes series in 1978; Alderman, however, was to make a big splash in 1981 and along with Geoff Lawson would be a huge part of Australian Ashes success.

We were bowled out for 185, which could have been considerably lower were it not for the flashing blade of Graham Dilley. Little did he know that wasn't to be the only time his batting would be crucial that summer.

We had the Aussies on the rack by the close, though, on 33–4, showing just how good a day it was for bowling and causing me to be very satisfied with our position going into day two. The Aussies should have been done for on a day similar to the first in terms of difficulty to bat, but instead of dismissing them for under 100 we dropped around six catches to let them off the hook and get within six runs of our total. I would have liked to have read the Riot Act to those who dropped their catches, but when three of them were put down by me I thought I wasn't quite on solid ground from which to complain. Why did I drop so many catches when I had one of the safest pairs of hands in the game? I'm not quite sure, but perhaps my mind was on other things and it was having a knock-on effect on my cricket.

In any case, with parity in the first innings, the game was all about building a big lead for the Aussies to chase, yet by the time we had extended the lead to 19 we had already lost Gooch, Boycott and Bob Woolmer. The late Bob Woolmer was a top-notch cricketer who was just about the friendliest man I knew in the game. He was such a peaceful chap, constantly smiling and enjoying himself no matter what the situation. His tragic death in the Caribbean during the 2007 World Cup was a very difficult time for everyone in the game who knew him. Back in 1981, he was very much a part of my and England's plan to retain the Ashes.

By the close of the third day, we had lost six wickets and our lead was only 100. I was still there and although it wasn't my natural sort of knock, I was trying to convince myself that I was back in some kind of form with the bat. When I was out for 33, however, it was clear that I wasn't. Needing 132 to win, Australia still had to work hard to get there, but they managed it by four wickets on the first-ever Sunday of Test cricket in England. Clearly, somebody disagreed with the principle and we were 0–1 down. I made that joke to a couple of the cricket writers when they found me later on, and their averted eyes told me they didn't think divine intervention had much to do with the defeat.

I was taken to one side by Alec Bedser again at the close of the match and he told me that I was still England captain – just. I'd have one more match, at Lord's, to see if I could get things right. My mood was so low at Trent Bridge that I don't think it felt like particularly good news, really.

I've never been one to feel sorry for myself, but being captain was dragging me down and, as always, Kath was having to bear the brunt of my bad moods. The job that I had wanted to do so badly ever since becoming a professional cricketer was suffocating me, but I couldn't bring myself to do anything about it. I just thought it would be all right if I kept at it, that I was bound to come good sooner or later. Oh, how wrong I was.

The second Test at Lord's was the next chapter in my trial as England captain, and everything I or anyone else to do with the England team did, the press related directly to the impact it would have on my captaincy career. In a book he'd recently written, Bob Willis discussed his opinion that I had been given the captaincy too early against the West Indies, and it was completely taken out of context to suggest that he thought I was a bad captain when that wasn't what he'd said. I know for a fact that Bob would not have hesitated in giving me his full opinion to my face, so I know he wouldn't have done so behind my back. In any case, he is entitled to say what he thinks, as we all are. But this was an example of the media turning everything into a saga about my leadership.

By the time the game actually arrived, I didn't know what to make of it all and just had to try to remain focused on the job in hand. Fortunately, Boycs was playing in his 100th Test match for England and much of the attention was on him in the run-up to the game, which eased the pressure a little on me, and I was grateful for the way he dealt with questions on my captaincy. He could have had a little dig here or there, but he made it clear he was fully behind me out on the field. Whether he thought the same privately might be another matter, but he was good as gold in public and that was what mattered.

I can remember talking with Kim Hughes before the toss about the ground and the conditions. The sheer happiness with which he went to toss up was in complete contrast to my mood. At the time, I would have given anything to have one in the win column and it was with that in mind that I went back into the changing-room after being inserted and got our boys going.

My rallying call certainly seemed to work on Goochie, who went out there and played like a god from the start, while Boycs offered his usual staunch support.

Goochie raced along to 44, dishing out plenty of punishment to DK, but by hitting him out of the attack he actually opened the door to the younger and quicker Geoff Lawson, who caught him by surprise with a short ball that he could only hook to square leg. The rest of the top order were all accounted for by Lawson, while Bob Woolmer retired hurt with a badly bruised arm, but a brave knock of 59 from Mike Gatting meant our 191–4 at the close wasn't too bad. It was bad enough, though, for some writers to talk about what Keith Fletcher was up to captaining Essex and whether he could come straight into the side as captain to replace me.

The second day turned our way as Embers and Peter Willey both got runs to help lift us to 311 all out. I had been trapped lbw by Lawson for a duck, even though I thought it was easily slipping down the leg side.

With the rain and overcast skies, we had lost a fair bit of play that day, so when Australia had started their innings and we went off again at 7 p.m., I checked with the umpires that that was the end of play because we were already into the extra hour. They agreed, so the players all got on with their showers only to find out that minutes later the ground was bathed in sunlight and the punters were expecting more cricket. There was nothing to be done, the game was up, but because of some duff information on the tannoy, saying play could go on right up until 7.30 p.m., the crowd grew restless, and not for the first time at the famous old ground. I looked out from the balcony and could see plenty of cushions, the kind I used to sell, being hurled across the ground by fans, and a few members too, in protest. It wasn't that we didn't want to play; it was the regulations! I thought their behaviour was pretty poor that day, but that was nothing compared to what was to come.

By the end of day three, Australia had made it to 253–6 and, with a rest day ahead of me, I was able to take up an invitation to join one of Britain's greatest heroes, Douglas Bader, for dinner that night – only I didn't realise it would just be me and him until I got there.

I thought it was a dinner party for a few people, but when I arrived and was ushered through to meet him, it turned out to be a table for two, which was actually great fun. Douglas was a hero of our time, a Second World War fighter pilot and Group Captain in the RAF who had lived most of his life with artificial legs following a flying accident in 1931. And he was tremendous company. He really took my mind off things with his war tales and he helped put it all into perspective for me that evening. Here was this bloke who faced life head-on, much in the same way I always tried to, and he didn't let anything get in the way of what he wanted to do. If I'm honest, I think that evening helped me make up my mind to give up the England captaincy, if only because I realised that my family was more important to me than anything else, that my current situation was making their lives miserable and it had to stop.

I can remember telling him about my wish to become a pilot one day and my worry that they wouldn't let me have a licence because I was colour blind. He looked me up and down, then pointed to his artificial legs and said, 'Just do what I did: blag it!'

Thanks to Border and Hughes, Australia moved past our total on day four and grabbed a lead of 34 before we could bat again. My first thought was of how we could win; it was all about setting a target for the Aussies to chase and therefore giving us a chance of bowling them out.

Into day five and a decent stand between Gower and Boycott meant a declaration would have to be well timed. However, in the push for quick runs we lost three wickets, including mine for a golden duck trying to sweep Ray Bright, with the score on 217. The only reason I played that shot was to get the scoreboard ticking along; it was for no other reason than the team's success, so the way in which I was utterly dismissed by the MCC members on my way back to the pavilion stung me. Nobody would even look at me as I walked back and I felt like I was a common criminal rather than the captain of the country. It was an awful feeling.

By then, I had already made up my mind that I was going to relinquish the captaincy if they didn't give it to me long term, but that little incident was enough to confirm my feelings about my position.

THE COMEBACK

In the eleven days between resigning as England captain and the third Test at Headingley, I played for Somerset three times.

Can you imagine anyone doing that now? When Michael Vaughan resigned in 2008, he 'took some time off' after a tearful exit. Once I was out of the door at Lord's and had had the chance to speak with Kath, it was back to business for my county, trying to secure some more silverware to go with the one-day trophies we'd picked up in 1979. We had a Benson & Hedges Cup match against Kent followed by a county game and a John Player League game against Sussex, and I was involved in all three.

There were two reasons why I threw myself back into cricket. First, it was my job and it was what I did best, so there was nowhere that I felt more comfortable than out on a cricket field with my Somerset teammates.

I know I subsequently fell out with a few people there after the sacking of Viv and Joel, but at this stage it was a real sanctuary for me and it is something that the West Country community does better than most, I think. Just look at the way they have helped and supported Marcus Trescothick during his difficult periods. Sportsmen are not robots and we get affected by the same things as the rest of the general public, but because we play sport in front of thousands we are supposed somehow to be able to cope with anything. It doesn't always work like that and although I would say that I managed to get through plenty on my own – thanks largely to my stubbornness – I can appreciate now that going back to my county for those days to play cricket was a real help and made me realise that I had to get back on the horse for England quick smart too.

Somerset is a really close-knit club and in 1981 I was part of a fantastic dressing-room that gave me a hell of a lot of support when I needed it. There were guys in that side like the late Peter 'Dasher' Denning who were really great friends whom you could rely on to put a smile on your face, and they got me ready for Headingley.

The second reason I went back to Somerset to play was that there was a very real risk that I might not be picked for the third Test, and on form I probably didn't deserve to be. If I went back to my county and showed a bit of form, then, together with the freedom of not having the captaincy any more, I thought that should be enough to get me in the side. Thankfully, I managed to deliver. We won the B&H game by five wickets with a little three-fer from yours truly, before grabbing 6–90 in the first innings against Sussex and 72 with the bat in the second. We lost the game by six wickets, unfortunately, but I was back amongst the runs and the wickets and was itching to get back to face the Aussies.

Luckily for me, the England selectors went for a calm hand on the tiller and appointed my first skipper, Mike Brearley, for the next three Test matches. He had made it clear that he wouldn't be touring again, so the selectors gave him the job for all but the last, giving them scope to introduce a new skipper ahead of the winter tour if they wanted to. That made it clear that, with Brears' record, this was an Ashes-winning mission only – there were no eyes on the future.

His appointment ensured that I was given another shot at the Australians, although he nearly snatched it away from me the day before the game. We were at the nets getting a bit of last-minute preparation in when Mike pulled me to one side and said, 'Beef, are you sure you want to play? With everything that has happened, I'd completely understand if you wanted to step aside.'

I fixed him with a stare that said 'I can't believe you've asked me that', and I told him, 'Of course I want to play.'

His delight at my answer was obvious. 'Oh, that's great,' he said. 'I think you'll score 150 runs and take 10 wickets in this game!'

I'm not quite sure if he really believed that, but I certainly did, and I went into the game feeling as good as I could be.

There were two changes to the side that had drawn at Lord's, with Bob Woolmer making way for Brears to come back in and Yorkshire skipper Chris Old replacing Mike Hendrick in the bowling department. Chris knew the Headingley ground like the back of his hand and it was thought he'd give the side a bit of a local boost. Mike had actually been going to play in the game instead of Bob Willis – how history could have been different! Bob had been suffering from a bit of flu during the second Test and was only just over it. He hadn't played for Warwickshire in the county championship and so had to turn out for the 2nd XI to prove he was all right. Even so, Brears wasn't sure whether to include him right up until the eleventh hour, but had a change of heart and stuck him in.

Things didn't start too well for us, which had been the tale of the summer so far. The Aussies leant on John Dyson's 102 on day one, which gave them a platform on which to build a huge total. At 203–3, it didn't look great for us, and on the second day Kim Hughes' 89 put them on course for 401–9 declared, which gave them a few overs at Goochie and Boycs before the close.

One positive from the day was a return to bowling form for me. I took 6–95, my first five-wicket haul in a year. Already, my critics had the ammunition they wanted to suggest that the captaincy was what had brought me down and that only now I didn't have it could I play the way I was supposed to. I still think that wasn't the whole story, but as time wore on and my performances improved, it became received wisdom that Beefy couldn't captain and play well. It was the same argument used against Fred after he led England to their 5–0 drubbing in Australia. What about England's win in Mumbai under him and his five successive fifties as captain? They got forgotten pretty quickly, didn't they?

Anyway, our chance to put a big score on the board ourselves was snatched away almost instantly by a three-pronged Aussie pace attack that blew us away in under a day. D.K. Lillee, Terry Alderman and Geoff Lawson were all fine bowlers, but at Headingley that day they were match-winners. They shared the ten wickets evenly amongst themselves, but essentially we had no answer. Guys were either caught at the wicket or bowled as the Aussies got the ball to move off the seam just enough, and our first-innings total of 174 was just pitiful. To make matters worse, they enforced the follow-on and we lost Goochie a second time that day before the close. He'd faced a total of four balls on that Saturday and scored no runs for twice out! We were 221 runs away from an innings defeat with 9 wickets in hand. The game was as good as up and both sides knew it.

The bookies certainly thought they knew it. Ladbrokes flashed up the odds of 500–1 against England on the giant scoreboard. Everyone knows that DK and Rod Marsh, the natural gamblers that they are, took advantage of the generous odds on offer and sent their bus driver to go and stake a total of £30 on the bet. They had wanted it to be more, with a contribution from the team kitty, but were told to pipe down by the more sensible members of the side. The fact is, most people fancied a bit of it and Bob Taylor in our side made a beeline for the betting tent, only he couldn't get round in time due to the large number of people trying to leave the ground. That was one time the Aussies definitely outmanoeuvred us.

That evening, they had plenty to celebrate and they did so at my expense. Each year during the Headingley Test when I was living in Humberside, I would host a barbecue for both teams ahead of the rest day, which was always a lot of fun. I still do it these days around the Durham match, but without the rest days it is hard to get the teams along – although after a one-day match recently, I had the New Zealand boys come up and have a glass of wine or two, and they were great company.

Back in 1981, there was one team in high spirits and another not so happy. The Aussies were cock-a-hoop and they had plenty to smile about. Kim Hughes thought his side were going 2–0 up in the Ashes with just three to play, DK was celebrating his 32nd birthday and Rod Marsh's catch to get rid of me had taken him past Alan Knott's record for most Test dismissals. Meanwhile, the

England boys only had the possibility of an extra night at home to celebrate before what would surely be an early finish. The Aussies had a good old-fashioned drink-up, and as the night wore on a few of our lot joined in, not to celebrate but in acknowledgement that this game would surely be the last we all played together. Another defeat and the selectors would have been ringing the changes for sure, and I know that Bob Willis in particular, with his injury record, thought this was the last game he would ever play for England. That was why late into that night the pair of us were dancing together like a pair of honeymooners, sweeping across the floor. We got on very well, did Bob and I, so it came as no surprise to Kath when she saw the pair of us waltzing around the front room in a wine-soaked haze.

The following day, there were a few English and Australian bodies strewn across the house, but they were all good as gold in the clean-up operation. I wanted the house to be smart for when I got back, which I was so sure would be later on the Monday that I only drove to the team hotel that morning to check out before heading for the ground. It looked like a smart move as we went from 6–1 to 135–7 midway through the day. I was at the crease initially with Boycs, who had erected the original team bus in front of his stumps and wasn't letting anything through. It was so dull I cannot begin to tell you, *but* it was what we needed, someone to show a bit of gumption and fight, and that is what Boycs always did. He put the highest price on that wicket of his and, while others were falling to the Lillee/Alderman combination, he was steadfast. I actually didn't get off to much of a flyer, although compared to Boycs any run scored was up tempo. We had put 28 on when he finally succumbed lbw to Alderman, like most batsmen did that he bowled to that summer. It brought Bob Taylor out and he didn't last very long either. Now, I can't say that I had a huge amount of faith in Graham Dilley's batting at the time, but I did recall a knock he had played on debut where he hung around for ages showing that he was capable of batting, if only a little.

'You don't fancy hanging around on this wicket for a day and a half, do you?' I said to him as he joined me in the middle.

'No way,' was his reply.

'Right, come on, then, let's give it some humpty.'

And with that, Dill just took off. He went after everything and it came off for him. I was trying to pick the right ball to go for the big shot, but when I saw what he was getting away with, I upped the ante. I threw the bat at it in such a way that even if some of the edges had gone to hand, I think they would have broken some fingers and still gone for four! It was great stuff, real fun. The Aussies weren't too concerned to begin with because they accepted there was bound to be a little partnership at some stage but thought it would soon be over. I don't think they were expecting Dill and me to keep going and going and going.

After a while, it became apparent how the balance of power was shifting, and if I think about it now, the shift came too soon. The Australians should have been more relaxed about it, but they started fretting. Rather than one captain in Kim Hughes, they had about three or four people telling fielders where to stand. Each time I met Dill in the middle between overs, we were just smiling at the change in attitude from the Aussies. One piece of action I didn't take kindly to was the beamers Geoff Lawson slipped into an over. One I can excuse, but two was a bit iffy and I wasn't impressed at all. It didn't stop me, though, I just kept swinging the bat and the ball kept disappearing. I wouldn't say that it was my finest innings for England – it certainly wasn't technically correct – but what it showed was that I had a good eye for the ball and if I trusted my instincts, it could be very successful. I'd always been able to hit the ball hard, but usually in a more orthodox fashion. That went out of the window this time. Before I knew it, I had reached my 100 from 87 balls and by the close of play had 145 to my name as England had reached 351–9 and a lead of 124.

As I ran from the field with fans streaming onto it, I was as happy as I think I've ever been on a cricket field. I know we hadn't done anything yet and we could still have lost it, but at that point, with the crowd going bananas, I thought, 'This is what it's all about.' The guys in the dressing-room had stopped being teammates that afternoon and had become England fans again for the day and the unbridled joy in the changing-room just felt great. Even if we had lost, I think that day would have inspired us to something; as it was, we got to see its impact the following day.

There is a photo of me in the changing-room after my innings that evening about to light a cigar and it looks like I'm contemplating what I've just done as if I had any idea what it all meant. What was actually going through my mind at the time was, 'Does this mean we have to check back into our hotel tonight? I wonder if I can get the same room.' My mind was racing and there was no way I could comprehend either what I had just done or what we were about to do. It was one of those moments that I enjoyed so much, but it is only now when I look back on it and I can see where it sits in history that I can actually acknowledge what it meant. At the time, it just felt good to do my bit for England, for the crowd and for the millions of people watching on TV.

We ended up setting the Aussies 130 to win on the final day after Bob had got out and I was left 149 not out – my highest Test score.

We thought we had a chance on that wicket and if we got the ball in the right areas, but our greatest obstacle was Allan Border. He was their best batsman by that stage and if anyone was going to get them over the line without fuss, it was him. Mike asked me to open up with Graham Dilley, thinking that we'd both still be on a high after our heroics the day before, and also because Dill had a knack for striking early, while I could swing the new ball. It worked when I had Graeme Wood caught behind in my second over to make it 13–1, but thereafter nothing. Chris Old came on at the Kirkstall Lane End, and then after that Bob came on at the Football Ground End, yet nothing happened as the Aussies moved serenely to 56–1.

Now, if you're not familiar with the foibles of Headingley, bowling from the Kirkstall Lane End is where you want to be if you're an ageing paceman like Bob was. It is downhill and often downwind, so it is a bit kinder on the body. After a few overs uphill and into the wind, Bob was fuming. Here he was probably playing in his last Test for England busting a gut like a debutant, and he wasn't happy. I actually said to Brears, 'Why don't you let Bob have a go with the breeze at his back?' He smiled and said, 'Just give it time.'

With that, he switched Bob's ends and the result was instant. He removed Trevor Chappell with a vicious bouncer that he edged to the keeper before getting Kim Hughes and Graham Yallop in quick succession just before lunch. Those wickets changed the game. From 56–1 and cruising, the Aussies were tucking into their lunch with a little wobble at 58–4.

The pressure was back on them, but we had to get rid of Border, and in amongst the Willis wickets there was room for one moment of glory from Chris. He bowled the first over after lunch and managed to get Border to play on to reduce the Aussies to 65–5. The whole team sensed we had a real chance now. From there, Bob tore in and did the damage, bowling one of the greatest, if not *the* greatest, spells of fast bowling we've ever seen. He got Dyson and Marsh with short balls, while Lawson was caught behind, reducing Australia to 75–8, and we were practically there, but for Lillee. He'd obviously picked up a few tips from my knock and was swinging the bat, edging the ball over and round the slips like a pro. He got his side to within 20 runs of the win and the game was back in the balance again, but, showing he had a brain to go with his pace, Bob pitched one up full and DK could only spoon it to mid-on. If there was one man you didn't want to have to run in and take a catch, it was Gatt. As the ball went up, there was no way in the world that he was going to get there, yet somehow those little tubby legs of his went into overdrive, he took the ball inches above the ground and they were nine down. Poor old Ray Bright, Australia's jack and expected to win them a game that they should have cruised. He didn't stand a chance as Bob fired one through his defences and, with the middle stump gone, we had won by 18 runs, sparking the biggest sporting celebration in England since 1966.

It was just wild, pure and completely uninhibited joy. The crowd invasion was a given, and the boys were in seventh heaven, although Bob was in such a trance that he didn't even smile when he got into the dressing-room. When sportsmen talk about being 'in the zone', this was it for Bob; he had just taken 8–43 to bring about the most sensational victory, and he could barely smile. He should have been smiling at being presented with the man-of-the-match award following the game, but instead they gave it to me. I've always said there should have been two match awards in that game because we could not have done it without Bob. He was simply magnificent.

NAILING THE COFFIN

Where do you go when you've reached the top? Look for another peak and scale that one too.

Following our third Test drama, it could have been hard to get ourselves up for another assault on the Aussies, but, as people saw in 2005, there is nothing like a bit of high drama to get you ready for more of the same. In between, I played in a couple of one-day games for Somerset, one of which being the small matter of a Benson & Hedges Cup final at Lord's.

If ever there was a perfect time to be playing in a Cup final, then it was on the back of an Ashes win like the one we'd had at Headingley. It was around this time that I started to realise just what an impact that match had had on the country. I was in constant demand from all corners of the press and media world, not just the cricket writers. I was being stopped in the street far more regularly and my hand was getting sore from all the autographs I was being asked to sign. But I can tell you that I thoroughly enjoyed all of the attention. It was so different from what I had gone through as captain that I couldn't help but be happy about it.

I think it also showed just how much the country needed a lift like that. The late '70s and early '80s were a rough old time for the average person in the UK. There were around three million unemployed people in Britain in 1981, and that summer the country was still dealing with the effects of some serious rioting that had gone on in the spring. All in all, the country needed a boost and, as is so often the case, sport was a vehicle through which smiles could be put back on faces.

I had a permanent smile on my face because we were back in the hunt for the Ashes and there was a chance for some early silverware at Lord's. We were up against Surrey and, in truth, there was only ever going to be one winner. The reason was that we had the greatest batsman of all in his pomp. King Viv was simply irresistible and his 132 not out was worthy of a Lord's final. Throughout our time together at Somerset, Viv and I spent plenty of overs out in the middle, but this particular day, when I scored 37 not out alongside him to put on 100 unbroken runs and win the trophy, is one of my fondest memories, and I think it meant a lot to him too.

From there, it was off to Edgbaston for the fourth Test of the Ashes. I was in great heart, but that didn't last too long once the game got under way.

We won the toss and chose to bat, with Brears keen to get stuck in as our new opener and Goochie dropping down the order to try to find a bit of form. Brears did OK, hitting 48, but he wasn't exactly supported by his batsmen, who got starts but no one went on. To be skittled for 189 on an Edgbaston pitch that was usually a big-scoring one wasn't good enough and predictably we were labelled pathetic.

But when the Aussies batted, they didn't exactly find it a featherbed either and thanks to four wickets from Embers we restricted their lead to 69. The only problem with the success that our spinner had was that it gave the signal for their spinner Ray Bright to dominate their second bowling stint, and he delivered with 5–68. It meant they needed just 151 to win, which wasn't going to be easy, bearing in mind what had gone before, but after their experience at Leeds they weren't going to make the same mistake twice, were they?

Three reasonably early wickets put a bit of doubt in their minds, but by the time they got to 87–3, it looked as if there could be only one outcome. And by the time they were 105–4, it still seemed inevitable. Brears asked me to have a bowl and for the first and I reckon only time in my career I said no. Usually, you can't get the ball out of my hands, but on this occasion I didn't feel that I was the best option. I thought that

Peter Willey's off-spin might have a better chance of a wicket. It wasn't long, though, before Embers got the crucial wicket of Border with one that exploded off a length and landed in Gatt's safe hands. Well, I didn't need inviting twice with an end opened up like that. I told Peter to keep his sweater on and I was charging in.

Round the wicket, Marsh, bowled 'im! Steaming into Bright, howzat!! Lbw. Trying to tempt DK, he's nicked it! Keeper dropped it, no he caught it, no he dropped it, oh yes, he caught it!! Now into Kent, bowled 'im! And what about Alderman? Bowled 'im too!! Australia all out for 121, England win by 29 runs and somehow I've taken five wickets for one run in 28 balls and the victory champagne is ours again.

That night, Bob Willis was having a benefit dinner. The festivities went on well into the night and this time we were the side with something to celebrate: 2–1 in the Ashes with two to play.

What happened at Headingley was freakish, but Edgbaston proved to me that we'd got them. They didn't lose those wickets because I bowled brilliantly – in fact, the ball to get Dennis Lillee was almost a wide – they lost them because they were mentally shot. We had a hold over them and they just didn't know how they were going to win any more.

People have often come up to me and asked how I managed to perform so well against Australia and did I have some magic powers when it came to playing them. The simple answer is, of course, no, *but* when you play against a side like Australia, the contest means so much to both teams that the impact someone can have when things are going their way is huge. The opposition start to think about things too much and subsequently struggle to break that hold. Think about Steve Waugh, Shane Warne and Michael Slater in Ashes series, or Michael Vaughan, David Gower and Andrew Flintoff for England. At some stage or another, these guys have all cast a spell over the opposition, so that no matter what they tried it always seemed to come off. Flintoff's run-out of Ricky Ponting in 2009 is a classic example.

In 1981, it seemed like the whole country was enthralled with the cricket. Everywhere I went, people were obsessed with what had happened in the last two matches and it was partly because of that adulation that I made up my mind about South Africa.

The winter before, there had been a few tentative approaches to some of the players about taking part in a rebel tour, and, as England captain, I was one of the men on their list. It was a lot of money for the time and I was giving it some thought. When I had achieved what I had at Headingley and then Edgbaston, I think the desire to get me along took another jump up, but the reaction of the British public to what we were doing on the field really had an impact on me. If I chose to join the rebel tour, my England career would have been over, or at least curtailed for a very long time, and I simply couldn't bring myself to do it. The Ashes was so important to me personally, but as that summer wore on I could see how important it was to the fans too, so when the TCCB sent a letter round to all the players about what would happen to their England careers if they signed up, I put it to the back of my mind and set my focus on Old Trafford and what could be an Ashes-clinching win.

Again, I played a few games in between the matches, including a couple of rainy one-days for an international XI against a Durham and Northumberland side in Jesmond. It was part of a cricket festival that ran for about ten years and was a sign of the North-East's ambition to get cricket on the up. I've always loved that part of the country, but I had no idea at the time that I would end up playing for Durham when they finally became a first-class county. Their success story, from minor county to Division One champions in less than 20 years, is a remarkable one and I will always be glad of the small role I played in that during the 1992 and 1993 seasons, and even those little games as part of the Callers-Pegasus Festival added to it all.

Up in Manchester, the atmosphere was electric as the sell-out crowd expected more fireworks from their wildly unpredictable team. As per usual during that helter-skelter summer, we didn't exactly make life easy for ourselves. Another won toss and Brears got his pads on. We had brought Chris Tavaré into the side for one reason only: to shore up the batting at the top of the order, which had struggled to put a big total on the board. He did his job pretty well from the off, scoring 69 in a painstaking five hours, but yet again no one really hung around too long to make the most of his stickability.

When he finally succumbed to Mike Whitney, we were 175–9 and well short of our target, until Paul Allott shone like a star on debut to hit his highest-ever first-class score of 52 at number 10 and take our score to 231 all out. 'Walt', as Paul is known, was brought in to weave a bit of magic on his home surface, much in the same way Chris Old had been in Leeds, and this time he made way. Walt was a more than useful bowler for Lancashire and showed in the summer of 1984, when he took 6–61 against the all-conquering West Indians, that he had the ability to take wickets at the very highest level. By his own admission, his magnificent Lancashire career was never mirrored as a Test player, with 13 caps, but he can be proud of the role he played in the miracle summer of 1981. Since his playing has finished, he has been a constant jolly face amongst our merry band of commentators at Sky Sports, although his choice of shirts leaves an awful lot to be desired. It is colourful and exotic, to say the least!

With the ball, we fared much better, rolling the Aussies for 130, with Bob and myself sharing the bulk of the wickets. Our healthy first-innings lead was looking like it would be absolutely crucial in a low-scoring match, and when we were reduced to 104–5 everything was still in the balance. We thought we wouldn't need too many more to be out of Australia's reach, but we wanted to make sure we got there, so when I walked out to bat with Chris we were pretty circumspect in our approach. I know Tav got a lot of stick for the way he batted, but he was playing to orders so that those around him could play their strokes.

I waited until Lillee and Alderman took the second new ball and then began my assault. I went for my shots good and proper, and, just like at Headingley, the ball was flying to the boundary on a regular basis, only this wasn't the same style as my previous knock. That was a series of wild slogs that came off; this was real cricket shots being played by a real batsman.

I drove and cut and hooked like anyone should, I just did it a bit more often, and I don't think I gave the Aussies a sniff of a chance either. At that stage of my career, it was undoubtedly the best innings I had ever played and, looking back on it now, I would say it is still right up there. My double hundred against India was pretty special and my last hundred in Brisbane on the 1986 tour was an innings I'll always remember fondly, but I still think this was me at my best with a bat in hand. Three times DK bounced me and three times I put him in the stand for six. It was a blood-and-thunder innings, with a touch of refinement!

Chris stayed with me for most of the innings, and I have to doff my cap to him for doing the job he was supposed to regardless of the jibes he got for taking so long over it. Our 404 all out gave the Aussies a fanciful target of 506 to win, but in reality it meant five sessions to save the game and keep the series alive. Despite the dogged batting of both Graham Yallop and Allan Border, who both scored centuries, it was too much to ask, and, with the wickets shared around the bowlers, day five brought us a 103-run win and with it the retention of the Ashes. I say retention because even though the Aussies had comprehensively beaten us 3–0 in 1979–80, the Ashes had not been at stake as far as we were concerned, since it was only a hastily arranged series to celebrate Kerry Packer's securing of the TV rights in Oz. Sorry, Kerry, you don't get to play for the Ashes whenever you fancy it, old boy.

The celebrations were rightly long and happy. We still wanted to complete a 4–1 win when we got to the Oval, but I think it was tough for either side to raise their game high enough to dominate the other. There were hundreds for the usual suspects, Border and Boycott, as well as five-fers for myself and DK. For me, it was another personal milestone, as I reached 200 Test wickets and took 10 in the match. Our target of 383 for a glorious win was on the agenda, but a couple of early wickets meant we had to settle for a draw, with Brears grabbing a fifty in his last-ever Test innings for England.

It was a great finish to his Test career and spoke volumes for him as a captain and a man. Brears might not have been in Gower's class as a batsman, but as a skipper he was in a league of his own. He is still very modest about it all, even to this day, and he puts a lot of his success down to the players he had at his disposal. Well, as kind as it is for him to deflect the attention onto others, there is no question that English Ashes success in the '70s and early '80s was as much down to him as anyone. He was our Douglas Jardine.

At the back end of that summer, my life had officially changed for ever. I was always going to live life to the full, but as a result of what happened in 1981 my cup was overflowing, and it has been so ever since. I had a glimpse of what was to come when I was featured on the cover of American magazine *Sports Illustrated* in a country that hardly played cricket, and when Eamonn Andrews presented me with the 'big red book', I had joined some pretty illustrious names, although it was faintly ridiculous that they were doing it for me at 25!

While I didn't quite appreciate it at the time, that summer transformed my life and those of hundreds of people. It gave me and my family more opportunities than we could ever have dreamed of. It gave me the standing in British sport and society to be able to raise as much money and awareness as I have through my leukaemia walks and it provided something to raise the spirits of a downtrodden general public. It was only a bit of sport and a bit of drama, but it mattered. The Ashes always matters.

BOBBING UNDER

By the time it came to my third trip to Australia in 1982–83, I felt I knew my way around the place pretty well, and I was determined to enjoy every aspect of the tour, and not just on the field.

My relationship with the Ashes had taken a remarkable turn as a result of what had happened the previous year, but it wasn't all sweetness and light, as it might have seemed from the outside.

As much as I enjoyed the ride in 1981 from a playing point of view, I still felt hurt and angry over the captaincy issue, and I had also begun to feel the effects of 'tall-poppy syndrome', whereby people in the public eye are built up beyond all reasonable levels before being knocked down when the media and those in power realise that they are not dealing with a superhuman who has no faults or foibles.

I don't deny that I hardly helped myself at times, and I was certainly never going to allow external forces to stop me from living my life the way I wanted. Yes, that might seem a little selfish, but, as far as I was concerned, I had achieved what I had by being myself and it had been good enough up to now, so why not continue? You live and learn, I suppose, but perhaps it took me a little longer to learn than others; I've mentioned before that I don't consider the nickname 'Bungalow' inappropriate.

As we headed Down Under for what was, incredibly, our seventh separate meeting with Australia in six years, if you include the two Centenary matches, I realised that I had never been involved in a losing Ashes campaign, by virtue of the 1979–80 series not having the little urn at stake.

It had been a period of upheaval for the game and although the Ashes had survived, as it always will, there had been a feeling of unrest amongst the Australians because they hadn't got their hands on the urn since 1975. For a group of Aussie cricketers that included Dennis Lillee, Jeff Thomson, Greg Chappell and Rod Marsh, this wasn't really good enough, and they knew it. There was a general feeling amongst their group that the era should have belonged to Australia and the events of 1981 had spoiled things a little.

I could understand where they were coming from, because they had these established cricketers of great ability and they had been ambushed by an up-and-coming group of players that included myself, David Gower and Mike Gatting. That is the beauty of sport, and especially the Ashes: you have to perform when and where it matters, and until this tour the Australians hadn't really delivered.

As a result, I knew we would be up against it from every side. We'd have angry cricketers on the field, boisterous supporters off it and, as it turned out, the umpiring throughout was simply a joke. They might as well have told us not to bother appealing unless all three stumps were out of the ground; it would have saved a lot of energy and it might have saved me a bit of money too!

I had enjoyed another decent summer before the tour and still felt I could have a huge impact on the series, but in truth my back was really playing up and I was finding it difficult to play and train. I hid it well from the England management and from my old mate Goose. As captain, Bob needed all the help and support he could get, and I was determined not to let my injury problems be another thing for him to worry about.

We started the Test series in fairly decent touch, with a draw in Perth, although for one Aussie bowler things couldn't have started much worse. Terry Alderman had enjoyed a pretty good start to his Ashes career with 42 wickets in the 1981 series, but thanks to a fateful rugby injury in Perth he had to wait until 1989 to have another impact. It's no mistake when I say rugby injury. Terry was a big bloke and could handle himself, so when a few spectators invaded the field and one of them collided with him, there should only have been one winner. Terry chased after him, happy to have a crack at a Pom at any opportunity, and rugby-tackled him to the ground. The only problem was that he dislocated his right shoulder in the process and was laid out for the rest of the season. It was pointed out to him on or two occasions that he should have waited until he got to the MCG – the home of Melbourne's Aussie rules teams – before he launched himself, but he wouldn't listen!

In the game itself, Derek Randall hit another hundred against the Aussies in the second innings in response to Greg Chappell's first-innings ton. In a big-scoring game, the chances of a result were negligible, but I enjoyed two personal landmarks. I scored my 3,000th Test run when I made four in the first innings and when I got the wicket of Allan Border he became the 250th victim of my career. They were nice milestones to reach, but from that point on the tour went downhill for me and the team.

We went on to Brisbane for the second Test and we simply didn't do ourselves justice in the face of a hostile Australian onslaught – and that was despite the lack of D.K. Lillee in their side. He had to have a knee operation and missed out on the rest of the series. Unbeknown to him and to us, we would never have to face Dennis Lillee in Ashes combat again. Rest assured, if we'd known that, there would have been a collective sigh of relief not just from the England dressing-room in Brisbane, but from every England batsman who ever faced or thought they would have to face him. He was a true Australian Ashes champion.

Despite the lack of Lillee, Australia still had a rejuvenated Jeff Thomson in their ranks; he was bowling plenty of no-balls but the good balls he bowled were seriously quick. He formed a formidable partnership with Geoff Lawson and the 16 wickets they shared in the match were enough to put us 1–0 down. Kepler Wessels, the South African who qualified for Australia on residency, made an astonishing debut, with 162 the first time he ever walked out to bat in a Test match. It was his knock that gave them control, and the bowlers finished us off. Bob bowled magnificently in the first innings to take 5–66, but it wasn't enough on its own and the simple fact was that our batting let us down. We were missing a few players because of the rebel tour to South Africa, including Graham Gooch, and without him at the top of the order we were badly exposed.

Chris Tavaré tried his level best, as did Graeme Fowler and Geoff Cook, but we just never got a decent start with the bat, which reflected the quality of the opening bowlers we were up against. But at Brisbane, we didn't do ourselves any favours. Nineteen of the wickets fell to catches, which highlights a certain amount of batsman error. It was particularly irritating for me, when I should have had Kepler caught for 15 in the gully, but we put the chance down and with it went our hopes of avoiding defeat.

Heading to Adelaide, we had to hit back almost immediately if we were to stop the Aussies from running away with the series. I knew a few of the Aussie boys quite well by then and in private they felt they now had the wood over us out in the middle. I gave it my usual bluster and defiance back to them, but deep down I thought they might have a point. We weren't really getting enough out of our senior players, myself included, and without the experienced guys leading, the new boys didn't really have anyone to follow.

At Adelaide, we struggled from the off. I have to concede that I told Goose, 'If you win the toss, bowl first.' He took me at my word and as the heat increased to unbearable levels, with Greg Chappell batting like a dream, he directed daggers at me throughout our time in the field. Sorry, Bob!

With 438 on the board, we wanted to get somewhere near parity, but instead we were rock-and-rolled for just 216 and were made to follow on. In the end, their target of 83 was hardly an issue and they took a giant stride towards reclaiming the Ashes with an eight-wicket win.

This was a real low point for me and the team. We were 2–0 down with two to play and it was hard to see where our next win would come from. My back was killing me and I could see Goose was at a bit of a low ebb too. There was only one thing for it, and that was a rousing lads' night out to drown our sorrows and enjoy each other's company, a bit of team bonding, if you will.

I was sharing a room with Vic Marks at the time and my old teammate from Somerset was in total agreement with me, although I might have had him in a headlock at the time, so I don't think he had much choice. We had stumbled across a bit of a concoction out there that was essentially whisky and ice cream put into a big jug, mixed together and enjoyed with a little cherry on top. I rounded all the boys up, got them down to the bar and started ordering. There were a few glum faces to begin with as people were still to get over the defeat, but as the night wore on the boys became more and more relaxed and really started to enjoy themselves.

There were a few other people in the bar, including a few girls in some rather short skirts. Now, I can't remember exactly how it came about, but before long someone had a bet with Derek Randall that he couldn't persuade one of the girls to change clothes with him. Always up for a laugh, Arkle happily agreed and a five-pound wager was on the table. He went over to chat to the girls and somehow a few minutes later he tottered up to our table in full lady's dress and the boys were in stitches.

I got back to mixing the drinks and the next thing I knew, the lads were at the window pointing and laughing. I looked up and there was Arkle in full drag get-up walking across the street. I thought I was seeing things, but there he was in full view of everyone as if he was looking to get picked up. We didn't see Arkle again for another half an hour, and, to be honest, everyone was glad of the break! When he did come back, he told us that he had indeed managed to get picked up, by an Aussie whom he'd thought was in on a gag with us. It was only when the guy drove off down the road that Arkle realised something was up. He told us the bloke had put his hand on his knee, so he had to hit him with his handbag! The downside was that he then had a bit of a long walk back to the bar.

The night was a complete success from a team-spirit point of view and Derek Randall once again proved how great he is to have in your team. One man who might not have viewed the night with such fondness, though, was poor old Vic, who found the cost of the night placed squarely on our room bill. When I said we would be splitting the bill down the middle as per usual, he looked at me like a startled rabbit, but to his credit his protest only went as far as a few murmurings and stutterings before he got his hand in his pocket like a good lad – and that was Vic.

We moved on to Melbourne for the fourth Test feeling the worse for wear, naturally, and despite the fun we'd had in Adelaide there was still a sense of worry over our ability to stay in the series.

At the MCG, we were faced with the usual raucous crowd. They had turned up to see Australia regain the Ashes for the first time since 1975 and they must have thought that was exactly what was going to happen as we were put in to bat and were quickly reduced to 56–3, but Chris Tavaré dug deep and hit a vital 89, with Allan Lamb grabbing 83 to give us a half-decent total to work with. I slapped a quick-fire 27 to add to the mix and our 284 had put us in the game.

The Aussies responded in kind, but we restricted them to just 287 to have things all square going into the business end of the game. Yet again, though, nobody in our team went on to make a really big contribution and a few starts, including 46 in 46 balls from me, took us up to 294, leaving the Aussies with a target of 292 for victory.

We were in a real game now. They knew it and so did we. Forget how well the home side had played before now, the Poms were fighting tooth and nail to hold on to the Ashes, and a rallying cry from our skipper Bob before we went out onto the field did just the trick for at least one of our number.

Norman Cowans had not had an especially great tour up until that point. Not many of us had. But, boy, could he bowl when the mood took him. He could be very quick, and accurate with it, on occasions and this was one of those times. He also got a bit of help from a wicket that had only been relaid nine months earlier.

The innings ebbed and flowed, with Australia holding the

initiative at 171–3 until Kim Hughes fell to Dusty Miller for 48 and the collapse began. Cowans ripped through their middle and lower order to take four wickets for nineteen runs in seven hostile overs. Supposedly on a cruise to victory, Australia had run aground on the bowling of Cowans, and by the time Jeff Thomson strolled to the wicket they were 218–9 with another 74 still needed. We were home free, since Allan Border had been batting like a drain all winter and privately told me that he thought another failure would see him dropped from the side, while Thommo was a walking wicket.

It didn't really bother us that the pair hung around for a little while on the fourth evening. It was merely delaying the inevitable, and although they had reached 255–9 with a day left to play, we knew we would wrap things up nice and early the following morning.

The Aussie authorities made the final rites a freebie for any fans who wanted to come and watch their side lose, and for some reason around 20,000 people turned up. I suppose we should have realised then that something was up.

Bob used himself that morning, along with Norman and a bit of Dusty, but nobody could find the breakthrough. Thommo was batting like an idiot, but somehow it was working. We thought he was bound to make a real mistake sooner or later, but he just didn't.

I reckon the thought of actually winning the game hadn't entered his head until the target became a little bit more realistic, but as they crept under 20 to get and then 10, the fear just ran through our team like wildfire. We couldn't quite believe what was happening.

We had the game won. It was Jeff Thomson, for goodness' sake – but we just couldn't get him out. By the time Bob threw the ball to me, they needed only four runs to win and, as far as almost everyone was concerned, the game was over. I certainly didn't share that view, and I'm glad I didn't because with my first ball Thommo slashed at one outside off stump and the edge flew straight to Chris Tavaré at second slip. Yet somehow it didn't stick. It hit him straight in the chest and bounced off him. Luckily, the ever alert Dusty spotted the rebound and snaffled the chance and, with it, the game. That was as relieved as I have ever felt on a cricket pitch. We practically had to win the game twice, and that is never a great feeling.

Once we were all smiles and back in the changing-room, I had to ask Tavs why he couldn't hold on to the catch in the first place, and he said that quite a lot had been keeping low as the game wore on, so Bob Taylor had said he had to stand closer in order to take the ball, and, as any good slipper knows, he needs to move up with the keeper to make sure he had a chance of taking the catch in the first place. Luckily for me, Dusty wasn't as confident as the others and only moved a fraction, so when the edge came, it was with a newish ball and that went through too quickly for Tavs to grab. I told him it didn't matter since we had won, but, of course, if we hadn't, I would have throttled him! On a personal note, that wicket also meant I had become the quickest to collect the 1,000-run and 100-wicket double against the Aussies, which was something else to cheer me up on what had been an increasingly difficult tour until that day.

Our win by three runs was the tightest margin of victory the game had ever seen, until the Windies did for the Aussies by one run eleven years later, and it was the most thrilling way to reignite an Ashes series that had threatened to be one-sided. After all the drama and excitement of 1981, the Aussie public wanted a series like that of their own to watch, and this game had given it to them. Even though they didn't like being beaten by us in that match, they felt like they had at least retained some honour by pushing us so close, and I can only agree with that.

It all meant we were right back in the series with one to play. We held the urn, so we only had to draw the series to retain it, and that was our plan heading to Sydney.

Australia looked to squeeze the life out of things by batting as patiently as possible to get as many runs on the board in the first innings as they could. They took their time, but a total of 314 didn't look overly threatening. I had made a bit more of a contribution to the cause with four wickets, but it was with the bat that we needed to fire. The batting, though, had been our Achilles heel throughout the trip, and again nobody went on to score the mammoth hundred that would have put us in a position to win the game. A pair of seventies from David Gower and Derek Randall was the best we could muster, and it just wasn't enough as we were bowled out for 237. The Aussie captain-in-waiting, Kim Hughes, cemented his position with an Ashes-clinching 137 to help put the game beyond us. Eddie Hemmings did a fine job as nightwatchman and probably deserved a ton rather than the 95 he got, but our target of 460 was never realistic and the game ebbed away to a draw, although the Aussies did try every aggressive trick in the book to get us out.

The Ashes were theirs once more and personally I was sick to the stomach at the sight of the Australian celebrations. Greg Chappell apparently burned a bail from the Test and put it in a silver cup to represent the Ashes, since the real ones never left the Lord's museum. It was the first time I had been involved in losing the Ashes and it felt just as bad as I'd thought it would. No, actually it felt worse.

However, despite the way I felt about the defeat, I thought that five Test matches' worth of competition meant we should offer our hands in congratulation to the Aussies and share a drink with them now that the battle was won.

It is something that I have held very dear to my heart throughout my career and life. You play hard as you can on the field, but you shake hands and have a beer off it. That is the way I was brought up to play sport and that is the way I will always be. It is why so many of my best friends around the world are blokes whom I've competed with, and there is no better relationship than the one I have with the Aussies.

After the Sydney Test, though, there were one or two players who didn't see things the way I did and refused to join me in having a beer with the opposition. I can remember Arkle saying, 'Those blokes in there have just spent the best part of a month trying to take my head off! I'm not going in there for a beer.' That was up to him, but in my opinion you're only cutting off your nose to spite your face.

I was still in a foul mood at losing the Ashes, though, and as a result I did have a bit of a go at the umpiring in the series. Some of it was a joke and it had got to me, as well as a few others, including Bob. The only thing is that I was foolish enough to make my remarks in public and they were reported in the papers. The TCCB slapped a £200 fine on me, which really annoyed me. I should have known better than to expect some support from my home board after what had happened to me in 1981, and as it turned out it was just the start of more run-ins that I would have with them over the next few years.

My relationship with the British tabloids was also at a low ebb and when they were looking for someone to blame for the defeat the spotlight inevitably landed on me. I've never really worried too much about what the papers have got to say, but the tour had been a real disappointment and it was a case of kicking a man when he was down. My back was killing me and I was doing everything I could to play and have an impact, but it meant that my training had taken a back seat and I had put on a bit of weight. I could still do a job, though, and I was still 'cricket fit', but the sight of me having a chat by a pool with Dennis Lillee with a bit of extra timber on me was enough to send the papers into a frenzy, claiming that the only reason England had lost was because I was too fat.

They also got the chance to have another field day on the subject during the one-day games that followed, thanks to a very funny prank by some veterinary students in Brisbane. I didn't really see the funny side of it at the time, but with a few years behind me, and having become too comfortable in my own skin to care, I must admit these guys pulled a stunt that they can be proud of.

They managed to sneak a small pig into the ground by sedating it and putting it in their cool box with an apple in its mouth. When the gate steward asked for a look, they just told him it was for the barbie, but it most certainly wasn't. If it had ended up on the griddle, I would have enjoyed it much more than I did. Instead, they scribbled the name Botham on one side and Eddie on the other in honour of our portly spinner Eddie Hemmings. With an Aussie flag tied to its tail, they woke it up and let it run all over the Gabba, much to everyone's amusement. I was in the changing-room at the time and didn't find it particularly funny, but rest assured everyone else did!

HOME SAFE

To call my life in the mid-1980s a soap opera would be asking an awful lot of the scriptwriters for *Eastenders* or *Coronation Street*. I doubt whether they could really match the wild stories circulating about me, a few being true but most of them utterly false. It was the price I had to pay for leading a full life on and off the field, refusing to kow-tow to the powers that be and essentially enjoying myself where and when I could. I have never allowed people to dictate the terms of my life to me and I never will, but there were times during those heady days when I came perilously close to spoiling it all.

Throughout that period, I had a couple of things to get me through, and those were my family and my cricket. When I look back on my life and the things I've achieved, I have few, if any, regrets – certainly none when it comes to cricket. Whenever I picked up a bat, ran in to bowl or held on to a catch, I did it to the best of my ability and I felt both in control and happy. During 1985, though, there were far too many things off the field that made me feel completely the opposite. I can honestly say that the presence of Australia and the Ashes as a focus for me that year were a godsend and without them I might well not be in the fortunate position I am in now.

People suggest that 1981 changed my life and made me everything I am today. Without 1981, you could argue that I would not have become the sporting icon I did, and to some extent that is true. However, I can say now that the two Ashes series in 1985 and 1986–87 were the two most important contests of the lot to me, because if it hadn't been for them, I just might have fallen off the edge.

I had taken the previous winter off to spend time at home with Kath and the kids. After the mayhem that surrounded me and the England team in New Zealand in 1983–84, commonly known as the 'sex, drugs and rock and roll tour', for obvious reasons, I thought it was time for me to step back from touring life, and I missed the 1984–85 tour to India. I wanted to spend some time with my wife and just recharge the batteries in readiness for a big Ashes summer.

However, people at home were just as keen to kick me as when I was on tour, and an unnecessary knock on the front door one evening from the fuzz resulted in my being hauled up in front of the magistrates on Valentine's Day 1985 on a drugs charge. It had been the smallest amount of cannabis, but it was enough for me to be fined £100 and therefore become a convicted man. For those of you who have travelled to America, you will know how hard it can be at times to get a visa and in my case it became virtually impossible. Even now, after all these years, I still have trouble, although my persistence has paid off at times, such as when my good buddy Ian Woosnam invited me to play a round of golf with him at the Augusta National ahead of the 2009 Masters. It was one of the trips of my life and I will always remember it.

Back in 1985, I had started the season with a bang thanks to my break, and I was determined to make sure my form would get me back into the England side, even though my pedigree should have been enough. The problem was that there were a few members of the Establishment and the press corps who thought England would be better off without me. It was utter nonsense, but sometimes these people have a voice and they use it. There were suggestions that David Gower's superb marshalling of the side in a 2–1 win over India that winter was enough to prove that the team didn't need me. They had performed well under Lubo, but when he returned home he'd got straight on the phone to tell me that he wanted me back in his team. It was a nice touch from him. He might have been one of my good friends, but he was captain of England and he didn't owe me anything. He wanted me focused on the job in hand, though, and that is what his call helped to achieve.

I knew that Australia under Border would be a difficult proposition for us. There was no more Lillee, Chappell or Marsh to terrorise us on the field, but they did have Geoff Lawson, David Boon, Greg Ritchie and the wild Jeff Thomson in their side, which meant a tough battle for us.

Having felt in good touch with the bat and my back not giving me too much gyp, I had got into the swing of things with Somerset and taken my chance to show what I could do to the Aussies in their opening first-class match of the tour. AB was in supreme touch in scoring the first of what would be three tons in successive matches, while I chipped in with a couple of wickets and a punchy 65 without too much fuss. As skipper of the Somerset side, it was the first time I was able to go out and toss up with AB. I was in a great mood and he was his usual chatty self – the 'Captain Grumpy' bit came a bit later (although very rarely when I was around) – and I think we were both enthused about what might happen that summer. AB was looking to start something as Australian captain, with a lot of his senior players now gone, while I was keen to re-establish myself in the English game and the England side, so I think positive cricket was always going to be the outcome.

By this stage in my career, I felt quite relaxed about playing the touring sides. I was established and knew what sort of ability I was working with. But this match reminded me of my first meeting with Australia a decade beforehand because I really wanted to impress and perform. I wanted to make sure I was back in the England fold in time for the first Ashes Test.

After Australia had scored 365–4 declared, I was expecting to see the same from our top order, but we were blown away by the pace trio of Thomson, Lawson and Craig McDermott. It was the first time I'd seen McDermott operate and he was lively, to say the least. Still, I wasn't going to crawl into my shell, and together with Brian Rose, who joined in the fun, we slapped the bowling all over Taunton in putting on 105 in about 15 overs. It just felt right and I knew in my heart of hearts it could be a cracking summer against this Aussie side. They had the usual fight and aggression you'd expect from any Australian sporting team, but I wasn't convinced about the depth of talent. Brian certainly found out about their aggression, however, when a short but extremely quick one from McDermott broke his arm and put him out of action for two months.

I needn't have worried about my international status, though, as I was named in England's one-day side to play the Aussies in the traditional three-game Texaco Trophy series, which they won 2–1. I thought I had played pretty well, especially in scoring 72 in the first ODI at Old Trafford, but the fact that I got out to Greg Matthews trying to reverse sweep him didn't go down too well. It was a productive shot of mine that I'd played hundreds of times in one-day games, but Peter May, the former England captain, pointed out that it 'was not a shot you'd find in the MCC coaching manual'. I couldn't agree with him more! I doubt you'll find Kevin Pietersen's switcheroo in there either, but I think I know what most people thought about that when he played it in Durham against Scott Styris: wow!

Thankfully, my form for Somerset throughout the start of 1985 was good enough to merit selection in the first Ashes Test of the summer at one of my favourite stomping grounds, Headingley. The talk of me possibly not playing had got back to the Australian team and AB always took great pleasure in pointing out that the Aussies would love to have me if England didn't want me. As much as I love AB and Australia, I know where my loyalties lie!

That summer had been a bit soggy in parts, which had an impact on the pitches, although I remember still managing to get a fair few games under my belt. And when I played, I felt in such good touch with the bat that the ball regularly flew to all parts, so, going into the first Test, I was determined to show just what England had missed in India.

Australia started well with the bat as Andrew Hilditch grabbed a measured 119 and dealt with a selection of bumpers from Norman Cowans and yours truly with ease. The pitch didn't quite have enough pace and bounce to trouble him, but I knew that he had a weakness against the short ball and was keen to exploit it in order to get another wicket. The fact that he played me pretty well was a credit to him, but the way some of the press went on about my tactics you would think that we had come to an arrangement before the game. Apparently, bowling anything short that might get hit for four was an absolute no-no. Well, actually, I never minded being hit for a four or a six if I got the man out eventually. You cannot bowl with the aim of not conceding runs; that is what one-day cricket is for. Test cricket requires the winning team to take 20 wickets, so, to be perfectly frank, I was never bothered how we got those 20 wickets as long as we got them. Anyway, although my tactics didn't quite work on Hilditch, they certainly did on Simon O'Donnell, who didn't exactly have a debut to remember. Simon has gone on to become a respected presenter and commentator back in Australia and whenever I go out there for the Ashes in my new role, it is always good to catch up with him, but back in 1985 I think I was the person he hated most.

It is bad enough for young English all-rounders who have come after me to have the 'new Botham' tag thrust upon their shoulders – just ask Dominic Cork, Darren Gough and Freddie Flintoff, who are quality cricketers in their own right. But imagine if you are the young tyro from the opposition who has been built up as the man to put the old Botham back in his place. That is what happened to Simon, who had performed well in the warm-ups and was in with a shout of making his Test debut. He has told me since that he made a desperate call back home to his folks to tell them that there was a good chance their son could be in the baggy green cap very soon and if they wanted to see it, they needed to get moving quick smart. They couldn't get a flight out until the day after next, which meant they wouldn't get into England until the morning of the first day at best. By the time they arrived at Heathrow, the match was just about to start, but thankfully Australia were batting and Simon wouldn't be in until number nine. They hopped on a train to Leeds, jumped on a bus to their hotel and then hailed a cab to the ground, getting there just as Australia had lost their sixth wicket, so Simon was the next man in. As he walked to the crease, the pride coursing through their veins would have been immense; no amount of jet lag was going to stop them from seeing their lad's first foray into Ashes and Test cricket. A journey to Headingley lasting more than 40 hours was rewarded with an innings of two minutes as he walked to the middle, padded up to one of my straight ones and walked straight back to the pavilion, with a bit of a flea in his ear, as well! If any young player wants to know how Ashes cricket can chew you up, just ask Simon. In fairness to him, he scored a respectable 24 second time around and got his own back on me in the second innings, and I bet his parents loved every moment of it.

I really enjoyed the game, thanks to a clutch of three wickets, including Simon's, in four balls to wrap up the Aussie first innings, and also thanks to a knock of 60 in the first innings, where everything clicked, a lot like it did back in 1981. I had strolled out to bat on the Saturday with England still 67 runs behind Australia just after lunch and instructions from Lubo to play it as I saw it. I think he wanted me to stick around with Tim Robinson, who had reached his first Ashes hundred, and nudge us into a lead, but I had other ideas. I was full of confidence because of the way I'd been hitting the ball that summer and after a few sighters I started to enjoy myself, first against Geoff Lawson and then poor old Simon. I probably should have hung around for a bit longer, but I played on to Thommo and was back on my way; England had a healthy lead and we weren't going to give it up. In the end, we needed to chase 123 to win, and with 31 not out from Allan Lamb we cruised home by five wickets and life was good again.

The madness going on in my life behind the scenes was in complete contrast to the serenity I felt out on the field and, sharing a few beers with the Aussies after the game on the Tuesday, I was pretty content with where my cricket was at.

I was back in an environment where I was being tested to the limit as a cricketer and I was coming up with the answers again. My back problem hadn't flared up for a while and I was looking forward to getting back to Lord's. It was a ground where I had largely performed well in the past and where I had enjoyed some good times as a young cricketer, but it was also a place where I was keen to prove a point to the old Establishment after my treatment in 1981.

The Ashes urn – what it is all about. I know the fuddy-duddies say it is not a trophy, but it would be nice if the winners got to display it in their cabinet.
(© Getty Images)

Ken Barrington, the 'British Bulldog', at the crease. He was my schoolboy hero and went on to become a mentor and great friend until his premature passing.
(© Getty Images)

Bob Massie was an instant Ashes hero with a dream Lord's debut. I was sat on the boundary getting my first taste of the live action. (© PA)

John Arlott added a richness to the game with his wonderful burr. He also kick-started my love affair with wine! (© Getty Images)

I always enjoyed taking Aussie wickets, but when it was a player as good as Boonie, it was even more special. He also faced my last-ever ball in the game. (© PA)

Cricket and cricketers have a lot to thank Kerry Packer for, but he weakened the Aussie side for a while. No amount of money, though, could buy him an Ashes series. (© PA)

I took full toll of the Aussie bowlers at Headingley in 1981, and Geoff Lawson didn't enjoy it much at all. I had a great time, though!
(© Getty Images)

I did my bit with both bat and ball in 1981, and there was no better atmosphere or feeling than in the five-wicket blitz at Edgbaston.
(© Getty Images)

D.K. Lillee was the greatest fast bowler of them all. A classic action, a nasty streak and the heart of a lion. I'm proud to call him my mate. (© PA)

Celebrating with David Gower has always been good fun, but I was never going to waste champagne on his curly mop! (© Getty Images)

Not even Allan Border would've guessed just what an incredible star Shane Warne would go on to be, but in 1993 he announced himself in the grandest manner. (© PA)

It might have taken 16 long years to get those Ashes back, but in the most thrilling series of them all Freddie Flintoff and co. gave the whole country a lift. (© PA)

From 5–0 despair in 2006–07 to Ashes glory in 2009. Andrew Strauss was England's leader and star man. He brought it all together and has the chance to do the same Down Under in 2010–11. (© Getty Images)

This time around, though, it wasn't me in the spotlight, it was the current skipper, D.I. Gower, a quite remarkably talented English batsman who was able to do things with a cricket bat that artists can do with paintbrushes or superstar rock performers can do with their guitars. Here he was leading the side in an Ashes campaign and even though his side had convincingly won the first Test, the fact that he had contributed 17 and 5 to the Headingley cause was enough for some to get on his back and say that his slump was terminal. The selectors were even putting him through the same nightmare that they had done me by refusing to confirm him as England's captain for the entire series. They would soon see sense.

The truth was that being captain had taken its toll on Lubo, as it does on everyone. He had marshalled a great win in India and was determined to do the same against Australia. I think some people were fooled by his laid-back demeanour and they thought he didn't care as much as someone like Graham Gooch, but nothing could be further from the truth. Lubo and I have spent almost all our adult lives together in the same team, whether it be for England or in the commentary box, and I can assure you there is no more determined man than David Gower. It just goes to show how looks can be deceiving. Thankfully, from the Lord's Test onwards, Lubo showed everyone what he was all about.

It began with a gutsy 86 in a total of 290, which we thought was a half-decent score considering the havoc caused by the young tearaway fast bowler McDermott. He looked to be in the mould of classic Aussie fast bowlers: big-hearted, skilful, plenty of pace and bundles of aggression. His six wickets broke the back of our batting and cleared the way for the Allan Border show. He just wouldn't budge. We tried everything at him, quick bowling, short bowling, swing bowling and spin, but he played them all with such ease that we realised we would simply have to take wickets at the other end as he worked his way towards a magnificent 196. That was exactly what we did, thank goodness, and for the eighth time in my career at Lord's and the twenty-fifth overall, I managed to take five wickets in an innings, which was a record.

It felt good to perform like that and I thought I was bowling as quickly as I ever had done too. These days, whenever a bowler takes five wickets, he tends to hold the ball up for the crowd to acknowledge his hard work, much like a batsman raising his bat for a hundred. It is something I like in the game because I'm not sure people realise how much effort goes into taking all those wickets, and bowlers deserve just as much appreciation as batsmen do – if not more, because it is bowlers who win you matches, don't forget!

In any case, I had a sense of real satisfaction at my accomplishment, but despite the generous applause I no longer had a great rapport with those in the pavilion. I was delighted too that my final victim was AB. By this stage in our careers, we had become firm friends off the field and ferocious competitors on it, so when he tried to hit me for the boundary that would have brought up his first-ever double hundred and got out, it felt instinctive to go and shake his hand and say well played. I think he appreciated the battle we had been in and he knew he had earned not just my respect, yet again, but also that of the English public. It was a spur-of-the-moment gesture that was captured by the great cricket photographer Patrick Eagar, and to me it sums up what Ashes competition is about.

With it being the Saturday and a rest day to follow, I took AB out for a few drinks that evening to congratulate him properly and also to give him a good night before his wife, Jane, arrived the following day. It was quite a riotous night in a London restaurant and bar, with a few of the other Aussie boys joining us. Having finished the day on 37–2 in our second innings, and with not one but *two* nightwatchmen at the crease in the shape of John Emburey and Paul Allott, it was obvious we were right up against it. So that night I made sure that the Aussie boys were well looked after, in the mistaken hope that they might still be struggling come Monday morning. As it turned out, I was the one who was struggling, hobbling into the dressing-room at Lord's nursing a badly bruised toe – not a drinking injury but the result of a wayward golf ball the day before.

Still, when it came to my turn to bat, a bruised toe wasn't going to keep me quiet, especially not at 98–6. This was the kind of classic fight-or-flight situation that I loved as a player. It would be easy to roll over and give the opposition a free ride to victory, but all that achieves is to give them more confidence. If you make life hard for them and turn it into a fight they aren't expecting, then you can steal some of that confidence away and, on the odd occasion, you might even just cause a shock. Until the last run is scored or the last wicket is taken, the game is still up for grabs and no one has an automatic right to the result. I have never given in – it is just not in my nature – and so that Monday I was determined to give it a go.

I strolled in to bat at number 8 with us 37 behind and staring down the barrel, but Gatt and I got ourselves up to level with the Aussies and after lunch made an assault on a lead. I remember hitting McDermott into the grandstand for six and starting to get a feeling that it would be our day. The Aussie players were beginning to get frustrated and in contrast to 1981, when they were simply angry with me for hanging around, I got the distinct feeling that they were almost resigning themselves to chasing leather for an afternoon, and then it was over. Bob Holland had been getting too familiar with the rough outside the leg stump for my liking and after padding him away I had a swipe and got caught.

With 126 needed, the Aussies got home safe enough to win by four wickets, but having snapped up their first two with just nine on the board, I was adamant we could win. I had just become England's highest-ever wicket-taker, moving past my old mate Bob Willis's total of 325, and with that I just felt we could go on and win. When Phil Edmonds got rid of David Boon to leave the Aussies 65–5, they were wobbling, but that bloody man Border stood in our way yet again and his 41 not out took them home. It was 1–1 and the series was wide open. I felt we had enough in the dressing-room to get past Australia, but I wasn't sure if we had enough to get past AB. I don't think it is an exaggeration to say that he held the key to their summer. Get Border and you got Australia, and everyone knew it.

Moving on to Trent Bridge, I found myself embroiled in yet more trouble, only this time it was on the field rather than off it. But to this day, I still cannot understand why.

The game started well enough for us, with Lubo going all French on us in a bid to win the toss. Only Gower, who drinks nothing but fine, stuffy old French wines, would come up with the idea of taking a ten-franc coin out to toss. I mean, really, who even knew what a ten-franc coin was in those days apart from Gower?! Anyway, that certain *je ne sais quoi* worked and we won the toss, allowing the skipper to bat on a slow pitch and he didn't disappoint. He had come into a bit of form in the defeat at Lord's, but here he was magnificent. His 166 was exquisite. It was his tenth Test ton and ended any debate about his quality and about who should be England captain thereafter. Perhaps the fact that he had been given the job for the rest of the series just before that match put him at ease. Whatever it was, his knock was a beauty. Unfortunately, though, we couldn't capitalise on it as much as we wanted to, so our total of 456 was good but not good enough.

In reply, Australia had simply to bat properly to get themselves out of follow-on trouble, which they did. However, the moment that should have swung the game our way ended up being one of the most frustrating and annoying in my Ashes career.

My old pal Arnie Sidebottom had already gone off with a freakish injury to his toe (which, unfortunately, left him as a one-cap wonder, when he was so much better than that) and Paul Allott had been struggling with a tummy upset. It all meant that, as the only fast bowler left fit by the Saturday afternoon, I needed to step up to the plate and do a job for Lubo and the side. I have never been afraid of hard work and my attitude towards life, sport and anything else that comes my way is just to do it – I suppose that is why Nike have been such good sponsors to me over the years!

So with the Aussies hovering around 300–5, Lubo took the new ball and told me to let 'em have it. I didn't need a second invitation. Graeme Wood and Greg Ritchie had started to build a bit of a partnership, so it was time for a breakthrough and the crowd sensed it.

They've often said that I could empty bars when I walked out to bat; well, with the ball in my hand the crowd used to respond too, and this was a classic example. As I sprinted in to bowl the noise was deafening. I found Wood's edge, but Gatt spilled it at slip. A few balls later, I had 'Fat Cat' Ritchie plumb lbw, but the umpire, Alan Whitehead, said not out. He claimed to have heard an inside edge onto the pad, which I thought was utter nonsense, and naturally the double teapot came out. Using the anger I felt at the injustice, I ran back in even harder and Ritchie could only edge it down Phil Edmonds' throat at third man. I ran off in delight at a score settled only to notice Whitehead's arm outstretched, signalling a no-ball.

Normally, bowlers would be upset at themselves for bowling no-balls, but I knew that I had eradicated front-foot no-balls from my game after problems on the 1977–78 tour to Pakistan. I simply didn't bowl no-balls, and here the umpire had called me not once but twice. To make matters worse, when I asked him how far over I was – the usual enquiry – he refused to tell me. Ritchie had made it down to the non-striker's end by then and told me he didn't inside edge the lbw shout either, so I let go a volley of expletives. They weren't aimed at the umpire, but it was easy to see what had caused them!

To get rid of the frustration, I bowled a bouncer at Wood, only for Whitehead to stick his oar in again about me bowling too many short-pitched deliveries. These were proper batsmen, for goodness' sake, not tail-enders! You can imagine just how annoyed I was at this stage, and yet there was more. Whitehead's final move was to warn me for running on the pitch. Well, at that point, I was liable to do something incredibly stupid and had to ask Lubo to step in and take the heat out of things, because if he didn't talk to the umpire, I would and he wouldn't like to hear what I had to say.

Tensions were running high and that reflected how much both sides wanted to win and just how close the series was proving to be at that stage. By the time we finally dismissed Wood and Ritchie, they had made 172 and 146 respectively, ensuring that the match would get no further than a draw and the series would still be all square at Old Trafford. I would get a fine and a warning for my trouble in this game, thanks to my altercation with Whitehead, but typically the TCCB waited until just before the final Test before giving it to me – by which time we couldn't lose the series.

There was not a great deal to report other than frustration up in Manchester. It is the wettest ground in England and it didn't change for us that year, even though we now knew that it was just a case of when and not if we would land the knockout punch. Because of the delays, Australia managed to escape with a draw, thanks to the eight wickets taken by Craig McDermott and the 146 not out scored by that little obstinate so-and-so Allan Border. I do remember taking the mickey out of Border by suggesting he was Australia's own version of Mike Gatting, which he didn't take too kindly to! Gatt had scored a magnificent century for us in the first innings, so it was ideal ammunition to use against AB, but, rather than make him get out, it made him more determined and he saved his side yet again.

As has been the case so many times, Edgbaston was where it finally clicked for us and where the Aussies could no longer hold on to our coat-tails. The game had everything: great batting and bowling mixed in with plenty of aggression and tension, not to mention a touch of controversy, which always brightens up a game, especially when the disputed decision goes against the Aussies.

To this day, AB still moans about David Gower's catch off the boot of Allan Lamb to get rid of Wayne Phillips, but, as I told him then and tell him now, that was not the reason Australia were hammered by an innings. That was down to the batting of Gower, Gatting and Robinson, plus the exceptional bowling of Richard Ellison.

Elly had played a handful of matches for England without doing anything spectacular, but over two weeks in 1985 he saved his best for the Aussies, and for that he will always be remembered as a fine England bowler. He never quite had the pace to be effective around the world, but as an English seam bowler he was top drawer.

His 6–77 first up laid the platform and showed the Aussies how best to use the conditions – it was a shame they didn't pay any attention. First, Robinson tucked in, then Gower and finally Gatt gorged himself on a run-fest in true guzzling style. Gatt's ton was the most brutal, but Lubo's 215 was majestic. There was no batsman I enjoyed watching more than D.I. Gower. He was the best English batsman I ever played with and this was him in his pomp.

I didn't quite manage to join in the gluttony, but my 18 from 7 balls was a cameo that all bar Craig McDermott enjoyed. His first and third balls to me disappeared over the ropes, while the fourth very nearly killed him. If it had made contact with him, it would have had to, because from the look on his face if he hadn't been knocked out, he would have made an effort to do the same to me! In the end, he had to settle for my wicket, but I had got my point across.

The Aussies needed 260 to avoid an innings defeat, but they crumbled like the slopes of Eyjafjallajökull mid-eruption. Elly took four wickets for one run in just fifteen balls to wipe out their top order, and crucially he got rid of AB in the process.

The win was really a formality, but Phillips stood firm for a while until he hit a ball from Phil Edmonds into the boot of Lamby and was caught on the rebound. There were plenty of arguments over it, but, as far as I was concerned, it was out. Coming from Somerset, where Brian Close used to position himself as close to the batsman as possible in order to get a rebound, I was used to it. I can remember a story about a catch rebounding off Closey's head and into the hands of Phil Sharpe when he was still at Yorkshire, whereupon Brian claimed the catch as his own to deny Phil the chance of taking the most catches that season!

We were 2–1 up and got to the Oval ready to regain the Ashes. Just like in 2005, we only needed a draw to secure the urn, but, unlike in 2005, we didn't play for that draw.

It was actually touch and go for me whether I'd play. Not only had I been handed the fine by the TCCB, but I'd twisted my knee playing for Somerset two days before the game was due to start. We had been having a rotten time of it that year, and in those days you went back to your county to help out when you could.

Anyway, I was not going to let a bit of a twinge stop me from playing in an Ashes decider; it was just too important for that.

I told Lubo I was fine to play on the morning and he did the honourable thing in choosing to bat when he won the toss so that I could give my knee a bit more rest.

This time, it was Goochie who did me proud. He put together his best knock for England that summer with a chanceless 196, and with Lubo cracking yet another ton for himself, the Aussies were as good as beaten by the end of day one. They had picked the wrong team themselves, going for the extra batsman when they needed an extra bowler to force the win. Their batting wasn't up to much cop anyway and a first-innings 246 with everyone sharing the wickets was a poor effort. Not for the first time, I could see an Australian side cracking before my eyes. Yes, they will fight you to the end, and, yes, every Australian cricketer has plenty of resolve, but that only goes so far, and every man has his breaking point. We had found that point in the 1985 Aussies.

Elly completed the rout with another five-fer in the second innings, and the Ashes were ours. The celebrations started on the players' balcony and many of you might remember the photo of me pouring beer over Lubo's head as Gatt fires up the champagne. I was actually primed and ready to do the same with that, but, ever the connoisseur, Lubo warned me to keep it in the dressing-room and not waste it, since it was Bollinger – his favourite. After the amount of runs he had scored that summer, I thought I would finally listen to him.

FANTASY TEAM 3

LOWER ORDER AND WICKET-KEEPER

IAN BOTHAM

Where would I have been without Australia? They were simply the lifeblood of my cricketing career, bringing the very best out of me time after time. Having made my debut against them, and met the Queen at the same time, a series against Australia was always going to be special for me, but the sense of history that went with those contests was what did it for me. You knew where you stood with Ashes cricket. You knew about the players who had gone before and you wanted to be a part of that folklore, because it was the ultimate test against people you knew so well. Above all else, playing against Australia was a lot of fun. The games were tough, often with an edge, but you could smile and share a laugh and joke with your opposite man at the end of the battle. Whether that is still the case, I'm not so sure, but I do think the relationship between the two countries remains as it ever was. One thing that is for sure is that this team would have the sort of fun of yesteryear rather than getting involved in the kind of over-analysis that surrounds the England team now – and I wonder which style the likes of Freddie and KP would enjoy more.

As a batsman against Australia, it would be about sticking my chest out and taking the game to them. If we were on top, I'd aim to stretch our lead in double-quick time, and if I came in to bat when our backs were against the wall, I'd try to turn the tide our way. What I wouldn't do, nor would I expect others in my side to do, would be crawl into my shell and not be aggressive. I don't think I've picked a side that would do that anyway, but that would be made clear in the dressing-room.

With the ball, the Aussies had better bring their helmets, because there wouldn't be too much stuff to drive from me and the rest of the pace attack. I used the short ball a lot as a player because although it cost me a few runs it would get me a lot of wickets, and with a batting line-up like the one we've got in this side, I wouldn't have to worry about going for a couple of boundaries here and there because we just might get one or two of our own. What I would love about playing in this side, though, would be bowling in tandem with Fred, because neither of us would give the Aussies anywhere to turn for respite. For some reason, the crowds responded to me with the ball as they did to Fred, and the atmosphere at somewhere like Edgbaston if the pair of us were bowling would be something magical.

Of course, the atmosphere in the dressing-room would be pretty good too, and there's no question which camp the two of us would be in. While Boycs and Broady would go off to enjoy a nice cup of tea at the close of play, I think Fred and I would be enjoying ourselves somewhat, with Lubo and KP not too far behind.

BOTHAM V. AUSTRALIA

Played: 36
Won: 16
Drew: 9
Lost: 11
Runs: 1,673
Average: 29.35
Centuries: 4
Wickets: 148
Average: 27.66
Five-fers: 9
Ashes won: 1977, 1978–79, 1981, 1985, 1986–87

ANDREW FLINTOFF

How can anyone not love Fred? He is warm, generous, funny and loyal ... oh, yeah, and he is also one heck of an intimidating bloke on a cricket field, so maybe the Aussie public might not like the way he roughs up their boys that much. However, he is certainly well loved by the Aussies he played against and has their full respect.

Fred is a great cricketer when it comes to the Ashes and his raw numbers don't really tell you why. He hasn't scored the hundreds or taken the five-wicket hauls that others have, but he has been a match-winner and he has done more to influence the outcome of Ashes matches than anyone else in his generation.

I think a decent test of a player is what the reaction in the opposition dressing-room is when they see that man's name on the team sheet. And in Fred's case, they were always grateful when he wasn't listed. Why do you think they put in their finest performance of the summer of 2009 at Headingley, when neither he nor Kevin Pietersen was playing?

Fred loved playing against Australia because it was so competitive and he had to give it everything to succeed, so much so that sometimes, as in 2006–07, even his all was not enough. You will never lack for endeavour and spirit from Andrew Flintoff. He doesn't know when he's beaten and he will charge in all day for his captain and teammates.

He is also an entertainer, which is something the game always needs. Fred clears bars, gets people through the turnstiles and gives viewers an excuse not to do the ironing or the washing-up: they need to watch him play cricket. Whenever I'm out with Fred, the number of people who come up to him and just want to shake his hand and thank him for entertaining them is quite incredible. They don't mind that he lost the Ashes 5–0 because they know he tried his best; what they want to do is say thanks for making cricket interesting for me, or thanks for an amazing summer in 2005.

And when he was on his knees in 2009, struggling to walk let alone run in to bowl, who was there mopping up the Aussie tail at Lord's? Fred, of course, and that is why I'd want him in my team. I would also back Fred to hit the ball the furthest out of everyone in our team. That is not a title I give up lightly, but some of the sixes that I've seen him hit should really have been twelves! There is little doubt in my mind that bowlers don't like bowling to Fred because he is so big and imposing. When he is playing well, there seems no way of getting through an over without being clubbed for at least one boundary, and that is a frightening thing for a bowler.

He was nothing short of a one-man whirlwind in 2005, scoring runs and taking wickets at will. I know what it feels like when everything is going your way; you feel in good rhythm, you're fit, you're confident and it's as if there isn't a thing you can't do. Fred shone like a beacon in that high-quality series, and when you've got a player who can perform like that with bat and ball, you know you've always got a chance of doing something special.

I've known Fred for a long time. I actually first met him when he was a 14 year old, at the Bunbury Festival, run by my great mate David 'The Loon' English, and he still has the same cheeky, friendly outlook as he had then. To watch him blossom into the world's premier all-rounder in 2005 was something to be very proud of, because Fred epitomises the best of English cricket. He got to the top off his own back, by doing things his way and not by being 'the next Beefy'. That has long been an unfair tag to attach to any cricketer following me into the England side, and I always told Fred to be his own man. We've had some long and frank discussions over the years and have grown quite close, but I've never once wanted him to try to be me, nor has he ever done so. I've been there for a bit of moral support when he's needed it, but he has been an original, Andrew Flintoff, and he can be proud of what he's achieved. Against the Aussies in particular, he was a world-beater.

FLINTOFF V. AUSTRALIA

Played: 15
Won: 4
Drew: 4
Lost: 7
Runs: 906
Average: 33.55
Centuries: 1
Wickets: 50

Average: 33.20
Five-fers: 2
Ashes won: 2005, 2009

ALAN KNOTT

Knotty was a complete one-off, like most wicket-keepers are, but he was also the most gifted gloveman I ever played cricket with. His ability to handle the spin of 'Deadly' Derek Underwood was learned on the Canterbury playing fields of the St Lawrence Ground and fostered around the world with England, and in this team they would make a crucial pair in outfoxing the Aussies.

Knotty was the only man I knew who took a skewer on every tour so that he could check his boiled potatoes and make sure they were cooked just right. Jack Russell took after him in the way that he had to have his Weetabix soaked in milk just so before he would eat them, but Knotty was the first truly idiosyncratic keeper I came across. He operated differently in so many ways, but it worked for him. When we had finished a Test match, everyone else in the team would either enjoy a beer or some champagne, depending on the result; Knotty would have a sweet sherry and a lemonade chaser.

I liked Knotty a lot because he never cost me any wickets when I was bowling, and when we were batting you knew you could rely on him to hang around. I would always pick a wicket-keeper whose glovework was top class, because I'm not sure you can put a price on taking every chance that comes your way. Ashes cricket over the past 20 years has been littered with missed opportunities that England might have taken on another day, and I wouldn't want to run the risk of giving Steve Waugh a second life, because he wouldn't waste it.

Knotty didn't just confine his oddities to food and drink. I can remember getting a few lifts from him to and from the ground and whatever the weather he would have a blanket wrapped over his legs so that they didn't 'seize up'. Knotty rightly thought that all the crouching down that he had to do made his legs extremely important to him and he wanted to take care of them, but I think he went a bit too far by having wooden blocks placed on his pedals so that he didn't have to stretch his calf muscles too much as he drove! Hardly normal behaviour, but then he also carried around a pillow with him for about four years just because, he said, it was a comfy pillow. I told him he could always get another one, but that wouldn't do.

The good thing about Knotty, much like Boycs, was that it didn't really matter who we were playing, his standards were regularly high. He didn't get daunted by the Ashes series or fazed by the increased expectations, he just went about his business almost in his own little bubble. But he too was a fierce competitor, and you need that against the Aussies. He would be our Mr Reliable.

KNOTT V. AUSTRALIA

Played: 34
Won: 10
Drew: 15
Lost: 9
Runs: 1,682
Average: 32.98
Centuries: 2
Catches: 97
Stumpings: 8
Ashes won: 1970–71, 1977, 1981

STEVE WAUGH

There is no question which man you'd want to bat for your life in a crisis. Steve Waugh could bat in all conditions against all sorts of bowlers, but it was only when his side were truly up the creek and it was all hands on deck that you saw what 'Tugga' was all about. I've lost count of the number of times that either he needed a score to retain his place in the side or his side needed someone to dig them out of a hole and there he was. He seemed to react best in adversity, which is a quality every team needs because you're not going to be 300–2 every time you play.

I don't think you could class Steve in the very highest bracket of batsmen, although his numbers stack up against the best. I never found my pulse racing when he batted, nor did I feel like he was particularly taking the game away from the opposition, but give it five hours and then you'd see that he had made a big impact. Where I think Steve Waugh stands apart is in his cricketing philosophy and the way in which he produced a side that not only dominated world cricket but was all-conquering. Some will say that he did it because of the talent he had at his disposal, but I would go further and say that he was the right man for the job, one who was able to get the very best out of the very best. It could have been easy for his side to rumble along winning most of their games without thinking too much, but he pushed them. He made them tough and brutish on the field and made no apology for it; 'mental disintegration' my arse, it was just boorish sledging, but you can do that when you're winning. He also came up with a plan to make sure his side won more than they lost by increasing run rates so there was enough time to bowl sides out. He took Australia to the next level.

As a player, he always seemed to be fighting something and I think that was necessary to get him going. He was fighting with his twin brother for a place in the side to begin with, then he was fighting with himself to cut out the impetuous shots that were costing him Test runs and when he was fighting with the opposition he was at his best. We can all remember the picture of Curtly Ambrose being pulled back by Richie Richardson because Waugh had wound him up by telling him to get back to his mark. He loved confrontation, and many found that uncomfortable.

Certainly, he made a big thing of English frailties when it came to the fight in the late 1990s and early 2001 as he crushed us in the Ashes. Nasser Hussain knew him relatively well, having entertained him at home when they were kids during Steve's stint playing cricket for Essex and Ilford, and Steve loved the Hussain family curries. But their relationship meant nothing to Waugh on the field, and he would take particular pleasure in keeping England down. In the record-breaking side that won 16 Tests in a row, he was the only player who knew what it was like to lose to England in an Ashes series, and that drove him on to make sure it never happened while he was in charge. It almost became a calling.

His hundreds at the Oval on one leg in 2001 and in Sydney in

2002, when he looked like being dropped from the side, were two perfect examples of his fighting spirit, and there is little doubt that if his side got into trouble, he would be at the front of the queue to sort it all out.

WAUGH V. ENGLAND

Played: 46
Won: 28
Drew: 10
Lost: 8
Runs: 3,200
Average: 58.18
Centuries: 10
Wickets: 22
Average: 41.54
Five-fers: 1
Ashes won: 1989, 1990–91, 1993, 1994–95, 1997, 1998–99, 2001, 2002–03

ADAM GILCHRIST

The greatest wicket-keeper batsman bar none is the only way to describe Adam Gilchrist. There have been better glovemen and better batsmen, but if you're looking for a combination, you won't find better.

When he first came along, I thought his keeping was just OK, but over time he got better and better. The proof of how good he became was not so much the record number of dismissals he had (until Mark Boucher reclaimed that) but the number of dismissals he had standing up to Shane Warne. He took 39 catches and an incredible 20 stumpings to make them the most successful spin bowler/keeper combination of all time.

Any keeper can take the edges when they're flying through from the quicks, but it is when you stand up that you have nowhere to hide, and I thought the way he kept to Warne was magnificent. He also battled with his body to take some of the most incredibly agile diving catches you will ever see.

To watch him bat at number 7 was like watching a whirlwind arrive at the crease, and by the time he was finished the fielders would be left standing around wondering what on earth just happened. His speciality was digging Australia out of a hole with freakishly aggressive counter-attacking batting. Once, he arrived at the crease with Australia 126–5 chasing 369 against Pakistan before making 149 not out to win the game with Justin Langer – and that was in only his second Test match.

He could also take a game away from you if things were just about in the balance, building on a lead in double-quick time; he had a complete licence to thrill. Who can forget his 57-ball hundred at Perth in 2006, which helped Australia regain the Ashes. I would have been sad to see Viv's 56-ball record go, but the way he hit Monty Panesar over long-on was as good an exhibition of clean hitting as you will ever see and it is why he is the only player to have hit 100 Test sixes.

Off the field, I've always found him a pleasure to be around, but his clean-cut image is something that others have not always had much time for, especially his crusade for batsmen to walk when they believe they are out. I doubt Gilly would have got too heavily involved in some of the nights out I enjoyed with D.K. Lillee and AB, but that is his choice and you have to respect it, especially when he is so good at cricket.

Perhaps his most influential Ashes series wasn't the 2001 campaign, in which he scored 340 runs at 68, nor the 2006–07 series, which they won 5–0, but actually in 2005, when England managed to shackle him to the tune of 181 runs at an average of 22.62. It was England's ability to keep him quiet that really turned the tide their way, and I firmly believe that if Gilchrist had enjoyed a remotely successful series the score would have been different – but he didn't!

GILCHRIST V. ENGLAND

Played: 20
Won: 14
Drew: 2
Lost: 4
Runs: 1,083
Average: 45.12
Centuries: 3
Catches: 89
Stumpings: 7
Ashes won: 2001, 2002–03, 2006–07

DENNIS LILLEE

I put Dennis Lillee in with the lower order because he could be handy with a bat at times, but there is little question that he was one of the finest fast bowlers ever to play the game, if not the greatest of them all. For what it's worth, I think he was the best alongside Malcolm Marshall. The pair of them were the most complete fast bowlers I ever saw and it is difficult to split them, but on his day no one could touch Lillee, and woe betide any English batsman who had the nerve to take him on when he was in the mood. The thing that just about tips it in Dennis's favour was his ability to adapt to any conditions he was faced with.

DK was a master of his art, and for him it was an art form. It wasn't just about running in as quick as he could and letting the ball go quicker, although he could do that all right; it was more than that. He could make the ball do things that others couldn't, he could get more out of pitches, he knew what angles to bowl with, he knew what speed would be most effective and he could get the ball to move, both in the air and off the ground. All in all, he was pretty useful, but what impresses me even more about him is the fact that he had to battle back from serious injury to do it. He had constant back problems as a result of a stress fracture in 1973, yet came back from that to completely outfox England in 1974–75 alongside his fearsome mate Jeff Thomson.

He was at the peak of his powers in 1972, when he took 31 wickets in the first live Ashes series I ever saw. I watched Bob Massie do all the damage at Lord's that year, but the bowler I wanted to see close up was DK. I got my chance to face him a few years later on the 1975 tour and when we came up against each other in a Test match for the first time, in 1977, we struck up a good friendship. Never was I more grateful to know him than when I was locked up in a Perth jail following a row on a plane when I had been playing for Queensland and he came along to get me out, bringing a six-pack of beer with him – a nice touch.

We had some great battles on the field and he was a tough man to compete with, but there was always a smile lurking behind his gruff exterior. At least if you gave him one, it wouldn't be long before he returned it, even in 1981, when his sterling efforts counted for little in the big scheme of things. He often asks me how his best-ever Ashes haul of 39 wickets plus 41 for Terry Alderman ended up being on the losing side – and before I can answer, he usually follows it up with a punch.

He used to have a very impressive collection of wines from Moss Wood, which is an upmarket vineyard in Western Australia. I say used to because he invited me up to visit him and try a drop or two during one of the tours after I had retired and I think he regrets it to this day!

Not only was he a supreme fast bowler in his own right, but what he has given back to the game subsequently as a bowling coach has been remarkable. Any decent young paceman around the world is likely to have spent a little time at his fast bowling academy in India, and his dedication to the art is complete. I have nothing but total and utter admiration and respect for Dennis, and I'm not the only one.

LILLEE V. ENGLAND

Played: 29
Won: 12
Drew: 10
Lost: 7
Runs: 469
Average: 18.03
Wickets: 167
Average: 21.00
Five-fers: 11
Ashes won: 1974–75, 1975, 1982–83

A TOUR TO REMEMBER

It was 1986 and it wasn't the first time that I had been in an England team labelled a bunch of can'ts, but it turned out to be the first time that we had the perfect response to it. We left England's shores a ragtag gaggle of no-hopers seemingly destined to be toyed with by the Aussie players and mocked by the Aussie fans, but we returned all-conquering heroes with the Ashes tucked under our arm along with any other bits of silverware going from a couple of one-day series.

From the word go, I should tell you it remains my favourite ever tour as an England cricketer and, as it turned out, it was also to be my last full tour with the three lions on my chest.

There had actually been a bit of doubt whether I would go on the trip, with a fair few dissenting voices claiming my off-field antics had got in the way of what I was doing on it. I had been banned from playing for most of that summer due to my 'revelations' in a newspaper about my use of cannabis (which was already known), and then when I slagged off the selectors for that ban at a private dinner for the amusement of the crowd, I was hauled up for an explanation, which luckily didn't result in them tagging on more time.

While all this was going on, England had endured a rough old time of it, with David Gower unable to get anything to go his way either as a captain or a batsman. His laid-back demeanour didn't help him and he was dismissed as skipper, with Mike Gatting brought in, but it didn't help things. The Kiwis were still knocking us about, and after winning the Ashes less than a year previously, it looked like we would be handing them back pretty soon.

Once my ban was lifted, I set about getting myself picked again. A lot of my credit had been used up and they certainly had no intention of dropping me straight back into the side, no matter how badly they were playing. I smashed a quick-fire ton for Somerset to help them win their third championship match of the season, and soon after I received a couple of calls from new manager Micky Stewart and Gatt sounding me out about a return. Gatt was tremendous during that period and beyond; he fought my corner when others wanted me out permanently. Micky and Gatt told me that as far as they were concerned my misdemeanours and indiscretions were in the past and that was where they should stay. They said they would be prepared to wipe the slate clean and start afresh, which was just the attitude I needed.

I can look back on that period now and reflect that sometimes when so many people are kicking you all you need is an arm round the shoulder and a bit of support. Perhaps I didn't always deserve that, but I was hardly the Devil, so when Gatt and Micky effectively did just that it meant an awful lot to me. Whatever happens in our lives subsequently, I will always be grateful for their handling of me during that period.

In the end, when it was clear they wanted and needed me on tour, I was only too happy to help. I was recalled for the final Test match against the Kiwis at the Oval and, with my first ball of my first over back in cricket, I took a record-equalling 355th Test wicket. As Goochie said at the time, 'I don't know who writes your scripts!' Neither do I, but that was a beauty of a moment because it let out months of frustration in one ball and the response of the crowd was nothing short of life-affirming. The great British public are often described as a motley crew and are told they are a broken society that needs fixing. Well, that is utter nonsense and on that day in South London I got one of the biggest lifts in my life when they cheered that wicket to the rafters. All they wanted to see was their man do well in an England shirt, and I was back.

The Ashes tour had been a real carrot for me during the

most turbulent year of my life and I was determined not to let the media or the administrators and former players push me out. If I was going to quit, it would be on my terms, not theirs. Besides, who wouldn't want to have another crack at the Aussies on their soil?

I think I realised deep down that this might be my last chance to do something special out there. I had had a pretty miserable time of it during the 1982–83 tour, when we were knocked around by the Aussies, and I felt that although I had enjoyed the successful tour under Brears in 1978–79, I hadn't been to Australia and played their strongest side and won. It was a little itch that needed to be scratched and I thought that I couldn't be certain that I would be in a position to have a big impact in four years' time, so this could be it for me.

I had been at a very low ebb at times during the mid-'80s, both on and off the field, and so Kath and I decided that we would be making the trip as a family, which was possibly the best decision we ever made when it came to touring. Knowing that Kath and the kids would be with me throughout the tour immediately put me in a much happier and more relaxed mood, which I think was reflected in the cricket that came thereafter. It was a huge cost to bear personally, but it became clear as the tour wore on that it was definitely worth it, not just for me but for the team too.

However, the tour did not start that well – at least it didn't look as if it did, not to outsiders. We started the tour with a defeat in our opening first-class game against Queensland before being completely outplayed in our third against Western Australia in Perth. There were two very good reasons for these performances. First, we had an interesting squad comprising some really young lads like Phil DeFreitas and some oldies like me. So from the outset the young lads were obviously going to take a bit of time to find their feet, while the senior players knew just how long and tough this tour was going to be, so there was no point in over-extending ourselves in games that didn't really matter. Yes, we wanted to get some decent match practice in, get a few overs under our belts and so on, but win at all costs? I don't think so. I'll quite happily take a spanking from each Australian state if it means I get to climb on board the plane home as an Ashes winner, thank you.

Another reason might have been something to do with the party we had the night after day one of the Perth game, when some of us were invited along to celebrate Australia's defending of the America's Cup in Fremantle. I enjoyed a pretty close relationship with a bottle of brandy that night and was just about as drunk as I have ever been in my life. Kath stayed back at the hotel with the kids and I had a riotous night with the likes of Gatt, Embers, Lubo and Lamby. I've always enjoyed myself to the fullest at various parties and engagements and I don't think there is anything wrong in liking a drink. Sometimes it just helps you to relax and put the stresses of life behind you. I would never have done something like that during a Test match or an international fixture, but this was a warm-up and there were lots of tough days to come.

If you panic and worry about things too much, I think that can end up doing more harm than good. Personally, I think that if players in the public eye are given a bit of leeway to let off some steam now and again, you will get the best out of them. I think people forget that we are still just as human as the next person and we need to be able to press the off switch too. In recent years, players have become almost robotic in their attitude towards the game and life in many ways, which I think is a shame. I don't think the early-to-bed, no-drinking-ever regime is right for everyone, and if you try to impose it, all you will find is that eventually something will explode, like on Freddie Flintoff's pedalo night – but more on that later.

Back in Fremantle, all I remember is having to be helped into a limo that drove me back to the hotel in a state, while Lubo managed to scrounge a lift off someone else at the party and found himself nabbed by the long arm of the law!

Apparently, his driver, who shall remain nameless, jumped a stop sign and was pulled over by a police officer. As David tried to hide in the back, his friend proudly boasted, 'You'll never guess who I've got in the back of my car!' Thinking he would be in all kinds of trouble, especially if the story got to the press, Lubo was less than pleased until he realised that the policeman was a huge cricket fan and just wanted an autograph before sending them on their way. I don't think he's ever been happier to scribble his name on a bit of paper.

The following morning, I was still in such a bad state that I got to the ground and dunked my head in a basin of cold water and ice to try to sort myself out. It didn't work. Spotting my obvious discomfort, Laurie Brown, our physio, took me into the treatment room next door and tried to revive me, telling the management that I had a bit of a niggle to deal with. Knowing that we were batting, I thought that if all went well, I would be able to sleep things off before being required, only our batting, unsurprisingly, wasn't up to much that day. Wickets kept falling at regular intervals and each time Micky popped his head round the door to ask whether I was ready to bat yet, he was told by Laurie, 'He needs another half an hour or so.'

We kept up this ruse until the score reached 69–6 and I had no choice but to get the pads on. I was swaying from side to side as I put on my gear, and even doing up the laces on my spikes had me taxed! Still, when the time came to walk out to bat, I took a deep breath and strode out with purpose, ready to make my mark. Imagine my surprise when halfway to the crease I got a tap on the shoulder and a voice said, 'Beefy, I think you might need this . . .' The twelfth man thrust a bat into my hand and off I went. When I got to the middle, the first three balls I faced from Bruce Reid all came down at once. I made up my mind there and then to concentrate on the middle one and hope that was the right one. It turned out to be a good idea because I managed to crack 48 from just 38 balls and be the innings' top-scorer, proving that a little drink every now and again is no bad thing for a cricketer.

We actually had a couple of decent nights out in the run-up to the Ashes as we took advantage of the hospitality of the locals around the country, and I can remember one time up in Bundaberg, when the senior pros could be proud that they did their job very well indeed – and I don't mean on the pitch.

After a game, we were in the back end of nowhere in this small pub, which for some reason that I still don't quite understand was called a hotel, even though there weren't any rooms. There we were having a few drinks and telling some stories when a few of the players noticed a group of rather attractive women. They sidled over to where the players were sat and started making a bit of small talk and telling the boys how wonderful they thought they all were. They claimed to be big cricket fans and were just so happy that the England cricket team had made it all the way up to their neck of the woods to play. A few of the boys were lapping it all up.

Now, it was clear to the likes of myself and David Gower that something didn't smell quite right. Here we were in a small up-country pub where these glamorous-looking girls just happened to be having a drink. It was a tabloid sting, clear and simple.

We told the lads one by one what was happening and sensibly they all backed off, but no one had told Phil DeFreitas. He was only a youngster at the time, about 19 years old, and he was in heaven. By the time he'd had a few drinks, he thought he had hit the jackpot and was quite willing to stay behind while the rest of us left. Eventually, someone told him what was going on, but he didn't believe us. He thought we were just jealous of his youthful good looks. Gladstone Small then asked him why on earth did he think these girls were there in the middle of nowhere dressed like they were. 'I thought they just liked their cricket!' said Daffy to howls of laughter from the rest of the group. His confidence took a dent that night, but it didn't last.

By the time we got to the first Test in Brisbane we had bonded quite well as a team, but our results had been awful and that is when Martin Johnson, the *Independent*'s cricket journalist, coined the immortal lines, 'There are only three things wrong with this team. They can't bat, they can't bowl and they can't field.'

At the time, it didn't go down too well amongst the squad, although we can all look back on it with a chuckle now because of what subsequently happened. But I think it was an example of how the British media can sometimes give you a kicking when you might expect some support. After all, when we go to Australia it is their players, their fans and their media against you. But that won't do for our cricket media. They have to be impartial, and if that means giving their own team a shellacking, well, that's what they'll do. For years, I couldn't quite understand why an Englishman would set out to rubbish the England team unnecessarily, but since being in the media myself I've been able to see it all a bit more clearly.

The English press has always been full of a wide range of characters, much like a cricket team. There are some great guys like my dear departed friend Chris 'Crash' Lander and Peter 'Reg' Hayter, not to mention his old man, the original Reg Hayter. Then there are those who revel in stirring and causing a bit of strife because it makes for a good story. What is clear is that not all pressmen are bad and neither are they all saints, and actually, on balance, it is right that our press strongly defends their right to call it as they see it. There might be one or two blokes you disagree with, but it is a free country and if you don't like what they've got to say, just ignore them. You need to let your cricket do the talking.

As a commentator myself these days, I would hate it if I couldn't say what I thought at any stage. Those of you who watch Sky Sports' cricket coverage will know that I don't really pull any punches. If something gets my goat, I'll be sure to let Lubo and the world know about it.

My attitude towards the media has definitely softened over the years, largely because I'm not too fussed what people have to say about me any more and because I know how the game works. But when you're a player, you can get caught up in your own little bubble and not really see why things are being written the way they are. I know that Johnno's turn of phrase upset a couple of players, but rather than bring them down it served as a motivating factor: they wanted to prove him wrong. We were already pumped up for the series, but by the time we got to Brisbane we were ready to explode, and that is exactly what I did.

The Gabba has become the traditional starting gate for Ashes contests in Australia and normally if you can start with a bang there, it is very hard for the opposition to stop you thereafter. With England having been on the losing side more often than not there, we knew just how important it was.

Despite having left Geoff Lawson out of the side and picked an inexperienced pace attack with just nine Test caps between them, AB won the toss and bowled. At the time, it didn't look like a howler of the sort that Nasser Hussain would later make at the same ground, but by the end of day one we were in control. That was down to the patience of Bill Athey and Gatt, who did a perfect job for us. Bill wasn't a certain starter when he came on the tour, and I think if Wilf Slack had enjoyed just a bit more success in the warm-ups, then he would have opened. As it was, Bill took his chance and gathered 76 steady runs as the Aussie bowlers struggled to find any penetration. I liked Bill a lot. He was a bit of a cheeky chappie behind the scenes and I can even remember him giving Elton John a bit of stick in our 'team room' during the tour.

Because I had the family out with me, I often had a suite at whichever hotel we were staying in, and it became the focal point for the team and their partners when they wanted to unwind away from the glare of the media or public down in the hotel bar. These days, the England side has a giant team room in their hotel that is decked out with table-tennis tables, pool tables, computer games and the obligatory physio's table, but that wasn't the case for us.

My room was the team room and Elton often joined us because he had a world tour going on at the time and was playing to sell-out crowds around Australia. Most of the players went and saw him at one point or another on that trip and he was fantastic, just one of England's greatest-ever songwriters and performers. With all that energy, he would have made a great fast bowler, if only he had a bit more height and could bowl! During that trip, he was giving it so much in his shows that he actually lost his voice and had to have a bit of time off, which gave him more time to spend at the cricket, something he loved. He actually changed his tour dates and venues to fit in with the Ashes tour so that any spare chance he got he could get along to the cricket, and it wasn't just a one-time thing either. He did much the same thing again in 2006–07, moving around Australia and dipping into the cricket when he could. I went to see him on that trip too, just after my birthday, and had a great time.

He's a big sports fan and it was a pleasure having him around. In our suite, he would be the one to get a party started after a game or on a Saturday night before the rest day. He became 'EJ the DJ' and took control of the music in the room. Because he had lost his voice, he'd been told not even to try to talk, so instead he had this chalkboard hung around his neck, where he would write down what he wanted to say. Anyway, I can remember Bill enjoying himself and asking Elton to put another song on, and when he put on 'Saturday Night's All Right for Fighting' (which I think is a pretty good song) Bill yelled, 'Oh no! Not one of yours! Put another one on!' It was all in jest, but I think I detected just a little bit of sadness in Elton as he changed the track! Both men were good to have around on that trip. Elton even babysat our kids to allow Kath and me to go out on our own once or twice, and apart from filling Liam and Sarah full of jelly and ice cream right to the brim, he was the perfect friend to us on that tour.

Anyway, in Brisbane we were busy putting the Aussies to the sword, but on day two they bowled themselves back into the game with two quick wickets that brought me and Lubo together. David was having trouble finding any touch in the middle to begin with, while I felt great from the word go. Every time I went for a shot, it came off and it put the Aussies on the back foot. It reminded me of my knock at Old Trafford in 1981, which up until that point had been my best Ashes innings. This one was starting to push it close, especially when Merv Hughes helped me to my hundred in double-quick time. He was a bit of a snarling, mulleted curiosity to me. I can't say that I was too impressed with his sledging tactics in the years that followed; in fact, I'd say they were pretty poor, actually. But on this day, Merv was my plaything, and as he charged in to bowl I took full toll, smashing him for 22 runs in one over. That turned the tide completely back to us and by the time we reached 456 the Aussies didn't really know what had hit them.

Merv actually received a bit of a sledge from me, thanks to an earlier meeting I didn't realise we'd had. He came up to me and said, 'Ten years ago when I was a young lad, I came up to you in Melbourne and said, "G'day, Mr Botham, I want to be a fast bowler. Do you have any advice for me?" and you told me I should take up tennis or golf instead. Well, what do you reckon now?'

I looked at him and said, 'You know what, Merv, considering I've just been smashing you all over the Gabba, I'd say that was pretty good advice!'

His moustache twitched in a manner that suggested he was about to smash me all over the Gabba, but instead he burst out laughing and bought me a beer instead. Merv got a reward of sorts anyway when his catch finally got rid of me off the bowling of Steve Waugh for 138. Unbeknown to me, it was to be my last Test hundred for England, in my 85th match, and it was a pretty decent one to end on, looking back on it now.

It laid the platform for a magnificent bowling performance from Graham Dilley, who captured 5–68, including the final wicket of Bruce Reid when the Aussies still needed another nine runs to avoid the follow-on. Second time around, Geoff Marsh batted like his namesake Boycott and thwarted us for more than five hours in compiling 110. It was the sort of gumption that made it clear the Aussies weren't about to roll over, and both AB and Greg Ritchie joined in the process. But as is often the case when you're looking to defend rather than attack, it is only a matter of time before you're on your way back to the pavilion and, rather than have the runs on the board that the time spent should have brought you, you've actually gone nowhere. John Emburey's patience was key and he just twirled away getting the odd wicket here and there, ending with 5–80 from a whopping 43 overs. It left us with 75 to win, which we duly knocked off for a seven-wicket win. So much for not being able to bat, bowl or field, eh?

We made our way to Perth for the second Test via Sydney and a game in Newcastle that got in the way of our first Test celebrations to say the least. We had certainly earned the right to enjoy ourselves for a few days, but unfortunately that meant being turned over by New South Wales in a game that served as a fitness boost for Lawson. He and Mike Whitney did the damage as we lost by eight wickets, but we didn't care because the main event was going our way and the Aussies hated that.

When we got to Perth, our game heads were back on and a good toss to win was taken full advantage of by our batsmen. Chris Broad would be remembered for his incredible efforts in this series, but when he walked out to bat on the first morning he had yet to score a Test ton, and Lawson was back to opening the bowling. It mattered not as Broad and Athey put on a magical opening partnership of 223. It was perfect Aussie-baiting cricket and nothing they tried worked until, just four runs shy of his own ton, Bill was bowled. We went about turning the screw on day two as Lubo and Jack Richards both helped themselves to centuries in our first innings, 592–8 declared. Inevitably, the man to stand in the way of the follow-on was AB. He wouldn't budge in another gritty ton that just about meant we had to bat again. In such a position of strength, the perfect scenario would have been a quick-fire declaration, but to be fair to the Aussie bowlers they kept the shackles on for long enough that we only had a day to try to bowl them out instead of the four or even five sessions we would have liked. They got away with a draw, but it was clear which team was in control and that put our squad in a great mood.

A.J. Lamb is a chirpy little bloke at the best of times, but following that game his gift of the gab went to all-new realms. We had a day off in Perth and a few of us loved a spot of fishing whenever we got the chance. I've enjoyed many an hour in Lamby's company catching all manner of sea creatures, but on this occasion when we rocked up to get our boat we were told that we could only go fishing in this particular area if we were Aboriginal. I was thinking that was the end of that, but Lamby piped up, 'Oh, no problem, I'm part Aboriginal.' I did a double take and Lamby just winked at me and carried on about his great-great-grandfather and how he had left for South Africa years ago but he, Lamby, was still incredibly proud of his connection with the Australian land. On and on he went, and I must say it was the finest piece of acting I've seen. He's not managed to reproduce it since, though, as you will have noticed in that series of Beefy and Lamby adverts that we've done over the years!

The only bad thing about that particular day was the laughter. During the second Test, I had strained my intercostal or side muscle while bowling a bouncer in the second innings and it was causing me a huge amount of pain whenever I laughed. The real killer, though, was when I sneezed and my whole body convulsed in agony. Laurie Brown told me it would be a painful rehab period and he was right. It meant I had no chance of playing in the third Test at Adelaide; my only hope was to try to get myself right in time for the Boxing Day Test in Melbourne. For those who saw the agony on Brett Lee's face when he suffered the same injury at Worcestershire in 2009, that is exactly what I went through. The Aussies call it the grunt muscle because it is the one that gives you the extra pace for your bouncers, and Lee certainly uses that one. It ended up keeping him quiet for the whole series, but I was confident I could still have an impact when I came back.

Without me in the side, the tour moved to Adelaide, and after seeing the pitch they produced there, I can't say it wasn't a bad one to miss. It was as flat as a pancake and as long as you didn't do anything reckless, you could score a ton of runs on it, as four blokes did. Chris notched his second hundred in as many games, as did AB, while Gatt and David Boon also got to three figures. A first-innings 514 for the Aussies at least meant they would have a foothold in the match. The last thing they wanted or would have tolerated was another collapse.

By not playing, I was able to take a bit of an overall view of things, which you sometimes don't see when you're immersed in the games, and I felt that the Aussies were kidding themselves if they genuinely thought that they had stopped the rot at Adelaide. While I was getting some intensive treatment for my side, I kept telling the boys that we didn't have to waste too much energy on earning a draw here because it was a good chance for us just to reorganise ourselves and go for a big push in Melbourne.

I spoke to Gatt quite a lot during that period and he was an excellent captain when it came to listening to his senior players and taking advice when he wanted it. In fact, I thought his management of the tour throughout had been superb. He hadn't pushed us too hard physically, like others had tried to, because he knew the best performances needed to be in the middle, not in the nets. He trusted his senior players to know what worked for them and what didn't; so as long as we turned up ready to play and could do our bit on the field, he was happy. He was just a very relaxed and easy-going captain when it came to his players, but he had a mean streak of steel running through his back when it came to the contest. Gatt never took a backwards step as a captain or a player, and although he had limited success thereafter as skipper, I thought his approach was right.

Having missed the third Test, I also sat out the match against Tasmania in Hobart, but if I wanted to play at Melbourne on Boxing Day – which I certainly did – I needed to prove some kind of fitness in a one-day game against a Prime Minister's XI in Canberra. I have to confess I was still in absolute agony when I played, but I wasn't going to show the Aussies any weakness. So, using a shortened run-up to concentrate on accuracy and swing movement, I played, taking two wickets and scoring 43 runs in a four-wicket win. As far as the Aussies were concerned, I was back and using my brain to take wickets, rather than hiding the pain I was in.

It was enough to convince the management that I was fit to play in the Test match, although I know they had their doubts. Sometimes you just need to trust your players to do a job for you in a match. The requirement for players to be 100 per cent fit before they will let them on the park these days is a nonsense. Just look at what happened when Freddie Flintoff said he was fit to play at Headingley in the 2009 series and they left him out anyway. A hammering inside three days would simply not have happened had he been playing. He comes back into the side to play at the Oval, and England win. It is not just about a player's ability to bowl x amount of overs, it is also about the effect they have on the rest of the team and the opposition.

We got to Melbourne in time for Christmas, and in those days the players and their families really enjoyed themselves. There is a lot less of the fun and games we had now because they are so professional, or at least that is the claim. Christmas is a time for fun with the family, no matter where you are or what the situation, and to lose sight of that is a big mistake. In 1986, we had a traditional fancy-dress party with everyone invited and it was a great night. Each person had to draw a letter out of the hat and whatever it was you had to come as something beginning with that letter. I can remember Bill Athey and his missus drawing out an S so they came dressed up as a schoolboy and schoolgirl, which went down well. Lamby and his wife Lindsay drew out an F and came as fairies, which I thought was appropriate. The funniest of the lot, though, was Daffy who drew a D out and came as Diana Ross! He had a huge wig on his head and a rather tight-fitting dress; the worrying thing was that a few of the lads thought he looked good!

Another great night of bonding was soon forgotten, though, when game time came round at the MCG. The Victorian fans had not come out in their droves and it was noticeable that the ground, which was usually packed with around 80,000 spectators, was only about three-quarters full. There was still a brilliant atmosphere, but I think we could sense that Australia were now on trial by their public. The results hadn't been great for a while and they were under pressure. The Aussies could forgive their side for losing the odd game here and there, but when it came to the Ashes, they wanted blood and the team weren't even getting us bruised.

We won a good toss, bowled and in the space of a day a new star was born in the shape of Gladstone Small. Gladdie had had his moments in a couple of Tests up to that point, but he hadn't played in that series and probably wouldn't have done if it hadn't been for Graham Dilley's injured knee. But you make your luck in this life, and Gladdie certainly took his chance. He got the ball to talk under heavy skies, and with Australia's batsmen blindly following AB's advice to attack, attack, attack, he made them pay. His 5–48 got rid of their top order, while my 5–41 from the shortened run-up accounted for the rest. Jack Richards took five catches behind the stumps, so we had made sure there would be plenty of people queuing up in the bar to get the drinks in after the game. Needing to avoid defeat to have a chance of holding on to the Ashes, the Aussies had almost coughed them up there and then.

In response to their 141 all out, we just had to bat sensibly

A TOUR TO REMEMBER

to take control, and there was one man whom you could have put your house on to do just that – who else but Chris Broad, who notched a third hundred in a row? I have to admit that I wasn't convinced by Broad before the tour. He had ability, as a couple of fifties in 1984 had shown, but I wasn't sure there was much else behind it. I was delighted by the way he proved me wrong throughout the Australia tour, and his hat-trick of Test tons was an astonishing feat. It provided the base on which the team could build, and Australia didn't really have an answer. If only Michael Vaughan had had the same support in 2002–03, who knows what could have happened there.

A lead of 208 was too much for the Aussies to challenge, although even I was surprised at their capitulation for 194, which gave us the win by an innings and 14 runs – and, of course, the Ashes.

I sat in the dressing-room with the England boys for a while after Phil Edmonds had taken the final wicket of Merv Hughes towards the end of the third day and I was happy. It felt like we had achieved something truly special after all the knocks we had taken prior to the series starting. My body was still sore from the side strain, but I honestly couldn't feel it because the elation at having beaten the Aussies on home soil for the second time in my career was so overwhelming.

I didn't know at the time that it would be more than 20 years and counting before we would win out there again, but it was still very special to me. The atmosphere in the group was tremendous and there was a sense of camaraderie among us that I'm not sure has been repeated on an Australia tour since – and maybe that (as well as the quality of the Aussies' sides!) has had something to do with the subsequent results.

I found out later that while we were lapping up the champagne in our dressing-room, Allan Border was laying the foundations of his strategy for the Aussies' future next door. Losing the Ashes inside three days in Melbourne had been the last straw for AB, who was still being personally successful and had grown fed up of losing. He made each of his team drink the beer they had and he told them, 'Remember what this tastes like, fellas. It is the worst taste in the world and I'm sick of it. I'm sick of being seen as a good bloke and losing. I'd rather be a prick and win. I never want to experience a hiding like this one ever again.'

Those were strong words from AB, but he backed them up with actions. To an extent, I think he went too far in cultivating a tougher approach at times, but what you can't argue about is the impact it had on Australian cricket.

It all started for him in Sydney during the fifth Test, although there was a Benson & Hedges challenge one-day series triangular between the two of us and Pakistan first – which, of course, we won!

For us, the celebrations in Melbourne carried on into the night with EJ the DJ spinning the tunes back at the hotel at a right old knees-up. Our little waiters for the evening were my nine-year-old son Liam and his seven-year-old sister Sarah. They did a great job until it was brought to my attention by Chris Broad that Liam had been celebrating a bit too hard himself and needed to be taken off for a cold shower to sort him out. It worked a dream for him, just like it had done for me over the years, and the following morning he was as right as rain.

Sydney produced a belter of a match and one that we shouldn't really have lost, but when the margin of defeat is only 55 runs and you get within an hour or so of saving it, you can appreciate that no side really dominated.

Australia had Dean Jones' maiden Test ton on home soil to thank in their first innings, while Gladdie backed up his efforts in Melbourne with another five-fer. I was pretty much useless throughout the game, going wicketless in both innings as the spinners did most of the work as per usual in Sydney. My golden duck in the second innings wasn't exactly a proud moment either. Looking back on it now, it is hard to get too worked up about it because we had the Ashes, but it would have made a real statement if we'd managed to keep the Aussies to nil and avoided giving them the whiff of confidence that comes from winning a Test match. It was the first time they had done so in more than a year.

We had another triangular one-day series to play before we went home, this time involving the all-conquering West Indies side, but they slipped up and it was us and Australia who contested the final. To cap off a marvellous tour, we came home with that trophy too.

When I got back to England, four and a half months after leaving, I was shattered but decidedly content. I had contributed fully to a successful tour and the Aussies were vanquished yet again, for another couple of years at least. I stayed in touch with AB thereafter and it was through him that I ended up playing for Queensland the following winter, missing the tour to India.

We got on in fits and starts, largely due to his dark moods and my determination not to be the Pom blamed for anything and everything that went wrong for the state. That period did strengthen my bond with Australia, though, and, without the pressure of an Ashes series going on, it opened my eyes to a bit more of the country.

ONE LAST CHANCE

The Planets by Gustav Holst is one of the finest collections of classical music you could ever want to listen to. I know this because I had plenty of time to listen to it while I was recovering from a back operation in 1988. By rights, my career should have been over as a result of the surgery. I was given only a 50 per cent chance of playing again, and at the age of 32 those seemed like pretty long odds. But I had unfinished business in the game and, as I always told myself, I wanted to go out on my terms and not because of injury.

The surgery was one thing, but the rehab was quite another and I must admit I wondered whether I would ever again be able to do simple things like kick a ball around with Liam, let alone play professional sport. But with time I got stronger and stronger, so that by the time 1989 came around, and with it an Ashes campaign, I was ready and raring to go again.

Thinking about it now, I was lucky that most of the dips and foibles in my career were intertwined with Ashes cricket, because I always had the impetus to come back and prove something. The Ashes became the carrot of my career, from 1977 when I was champing at the bit to make my debut to 1981 when I was in the doldrums as a captain, 1986 when I returned from suspension to make sure I got on the plane to Australia and 1989 when my back operation put my career at a crossroads. There is no question that I had a desire to keep playing cricket after that bout of surgery, but the fact that the Australians were touring the following summer meant I put an extra 10 per cent into my rehab work.

I've often spoken to Freddie Flintoff about his injury problems and how tough it is to keep getting yourself fit to play when the easy thing to do would just be to hang up the boots and say goodbye. But we both agree that there is no better feeling in this world than pulling on an England shirt and taking on Australia, and that is all the incentive you need to get through those dark days when it is just you, an exercise bike and the physio in your ear giving you orders. Fortunately for both Fred and me, that man has often been Dave 'Rooster' Roberts, and without him neither of us would have played nearly as much cricket as we have done. There may be some more from Fred to come, but even at this stage he owes Rooster an awful lot.

Rooster now assumes the role of physio and MC on my charity walks around the country. He seems to think that patching me up each evening after a lengthy trudge gives him carte blanche to come up with all sorts of gibbering nonsense in the support car that drives behind me during the following day. It is like listening to a bad northern working-men's club comedian, and the worst thing is that Rooster really is there all week!

By the time I'd got myself into shape and played a few games for Worcestershire, there was a fixture that I was licking my lips at the prospect of playing in. Our county match against the touring Australians came at the perfect time and gave me a chance to show what I could do. Once again, I was captain up against my old mate AB, just like at Somerset four years earlier, and the boys did not let me down. I say old mate, but during that game I got to see just how serious AB had become in the way he went about things. He hardly spoke to me during the match and when he did it was often just to growl and sledge me. It was a tactic that he was determined to use throughout the summer. I suppose by the end of it he was proved right, but I didn't like it.

It didn't make you any more astute as a captain, that's for sure; on a day tailor-made for swing and seam bowling, AB won the toss and decided to bat, thinking his men would get some batting practice in before the main event. Only he didn't take into account two of the county's finest bowlers in Neal Radford and Phil Newport, who took 18 wickets between them in the match. It was the middle of May and New Road was a bowler's paradise. Having skittled them for 103, we got a small but valuable lead of 43 and I managed to chip in with 39. Second time around, the Aussies got just past 200, thanks largely to a young lad called Steve Waugh, leaving us a chase of 163 to win. With a day to spare in the match, we won by three wickets. A useful 42 from me got people talking about my Test chances again and, considering that turned out to be the only first-class match the Aussies lost on the tour, I think it is safe to say we excelled ourselves.

I felt very comfortable during that game and by now was aiming to do whatever it took to get back into the England Test side. Quite a bit had changed while I'd been away, though. I had missed the previous summer as well as the previous two winters, through choice and then injury, so by the time I was in the frame again there was a new captain and a new chairman of selectors. It had been a miserable time for results, with the West Indians demolishing all who stood in front of them, and that included England, in 1988. Since the Melbourne win in 1986, England had won just a single Test – against Sri Lanka. Gatt had been banished from the job as skipper, and from the team altogether, for his bad-tempered row with an umpire in Pakistan and as a result of tabloid allegations about off-field misdemeanours, so David Gower was back in charge. Ted Dexter was the new selection chief, but to say that his methods were slightly bizarre would be an understatement.

After playing in the Texaco one-day series, I had hoped to be included in the Test set-up from the start, but a fractured cheekbone as a result of a mistimed hook against Glamorgan's Steve Barwick prevented me from getting enough cricket before the match to be selected. If I was fit and available, David apparently wanted me to play, but I had to wait a little longer before another Beefy comeback.

In the meantime, the genesis of the Australian dominance over England that was to last a decade and a half began in earnest at Headingley, where everything that could go right for the visitors did, and not much went our way at all.

The simple fact is that Australia knew exactly what they were doing and what their plans were, but perhaps more importantly than that, they had the players to execute them to the letter, and you cannot argue with talent. On paper, this was not an Australian team that struck fear into the hearts of its opponents, largely because it was full of players as yet unproven. Mark Taylor and Steve Waugh were two batsmen yet to make Test match hundreds, while Terry Alderman had never taken ten wickets in a Test match in his life. The fact that all three men changed those statistics over five days in Leeds is largely why England lost.

Perhaps if we hadn't stuck them in to bat first and allowed them to pile on 601, things might have been different, but our response of 430, built around a great ton by Lamby, should have been enough to at least secure a draw. All we had to do was survive for two and a half sessions on the final day and the Aussies would have had to question how they had managed to be so dominant and not win. It would have given England a great fillip going into the next match, much like the Cardiff rearguard action in 2009 gave them the confidence to go on and win the series. Instead, I have to say that we pretty much rolled over on that last day, and the defeat by 210 runs was a sign of things to come.

I still wasn't quite right in time for the second Test at Lord's, so I sent the side my best wishes, praying and hoping that the ground where England had not won an Ashes match since 1934 would at least be kind enough to give us a draw. It wasn't the first time that my hopes were dashed where Lord's was concerned.

England could call on the inspirations of 1981 *and* 1985, series in which England had lost the opening Test before heading to Lord's and then gone on to win the series. There was no reason why the same couldn't happen here if a little application was shown. Yet we shot ourselves in the foot a second time in as many matches following a won toss and a bad call on what to do thereafter.

In truth, I think Lubo was pressured into batting first because of what happened at Headingley. He didn't want to send the opposition in again and watch them make a huge score, so he ignored the overwhelming evidence of heavy, cloudy skies and a wicket with a touch of green on it to bat first, and the Aussies thanked him for it. At 191–7 things looked as bleak as the weather, but Jack Russell, showing the sort of gumption that any good old-fashioned wicket-keeper has, kept the Aussies at bay with a much-needed fifty that would have irritated them as much as anything, with his awkward, crabbing style.

No Aussie bowler really dominated, but the seamers shared the wickets around, showing that you just had to give the ball a chance to swing and seam and you could get wickets. It was with that lesson in mind that England's bowlers showed great grit and determination to haul their side back into the game with a spirited fightback on the second day. Graham Dilley, Neil Foster and Paul Jarvis were all tremendous that day and I can remember watching bits of the match on television and thinking, 'Christ, I'd better have my game in good order when I come back to keep up with these boys.' It looked like a proper contest out there. David Boon hit a pugnacious 94, while AB could muster only 35 before being snaffled by Robin 'The Judge' Smith off Embers.

At 276–6 by the close, the game was up for grabs. I'm only sad to say that the wrong team grabbed hold of it from there on in. We'd seen what Steve Waugh was capable of up in Leeds, but that was his first ton and anyone can get lucky. What we saw from him at Lord's was something altogether different and I believe was the first sight of what would subsequently become the hallmark of his career – the ability to dig his side out of trouble almost at will. I go into a bit more depth about Steve elsewhere in this book, but I think it is fair to say that his hundred at Lord's not only changed the course of that match but changed the course of Australian and English cricket for a generation – it was that important.

From being in a position to challenge for a win, England were left dazed and confused by Waugh's 152 not out, which included a superb marshalling of the lower order. He was helped by Geoff Lawson's high score of 74, but it was the rearguard action of Waugh that set the tone. He had clearly been chiselled out of the same Aussie granite as the likes of Bradman, Marsh and Border. Their total of 528 meant we now needed 242 to avoid an innings defeat, and, being reduced to

58–3 by the close of the third day, our options were limited.

Still, it was great over that third day to see Lubo stick two fingers up to some of the pressmen who had given him hell with a battling ton, while Robin Smith hit 96 in support. Lubo had got to the end of his tether during that game and actually walked out of a press conference early, claiming he had to catch a cab to a show that evening. Again, it gave the impression he didn't care, when it was because he cared that he couldn't bear to be kicked from pillar to post any more. I defy anyone to give of their best in whatever endeavour they choose and, after being given a bit of a lesson by their opponent, then have to take a barrage of criticism from those who merely sat in a comfy chair and watched their sweat and toil amount to nothing. It is no fun, I can tell you, so I understand why David got up and walked out. To be frank, if he hadn't, he might have said or done something even worse. I realise that it comes with the territory and is part of the job to explain to the general public via the media what went wrong or right out on the field, but what I can't abide is the seemingly rabid nature of the questioning when a bloke is trying to front up about his mistakes or failings. Where is the compassion or understanding then?

Anyway, despite their partnership, England could only get to 359 in the end, leaving Australia with a straightforward 118 to win, which they did, by six wickets, with Waugh again not out. I did wonder how we would be able to remove him from the crease by fair means.

Thankfully, he didn't last as long in the next Test, in which I staged yet another comeback – and I was desperate to help stop the rot.

I didn't really know Ted Dexter too well before that recall, and I was stunned when he thrust a song sheet entitled 'Onward Gower's Cricketers' into my hand and told me to sing it at the top of my voice to the tune of 'Onward Christian Soldiers' when I was lying in my bath that night. I thought it was a wind-up. I knew from my Aussie mates that they had taken this tour so seriously and had planned things meticulously, so the realisation of how amateurish the England approach was in comparison made me feel sick. It was all I could do to get the episode out of my mind before my 95th Test match appearance, something I thought I knew how to get ready for without Lord Ted's wacky ideas.

Just like on my debut, we were asked to field first, which immediately put me at ease, as I knew I could get into the game straight away. The fact that I had taken a wicket with the first ball of my return against New Zealand in 1986 had everyone on the edge of their seats as I ran in to bowl to Mark Taylor. I deceived him with a little in-drift and beat his inside edge to thud into his pads. It looked dead-set plumb to me, so we all went up in unison, fully expecting the finger to be raised, but no. Dickie Bird, great bloke and umpire as he was, took a little more convincing than most over lbws and he turned me down. I couldn't believe it. I had almost begun to believe that the improbable was probable where I was concerned, but this was a timely reminder that I was owed nothing on a cricket pitch, and why should I be? I've never shirked hard work in my life and I was going to have to work bloody hard to get any of these Aussies out.

It wasn't until my 13th over that I got what I was looking for, when Geoff Marsh was trapped lbw for 42. I was back. Alas, it didn't open the floodgates and, with rain virtually flooding the Edgbaston ground the following day, it took us until day four to finally bowl them out for 424. With the bat, it was quite a simple situation that just required us to bat properly and not give them a sniff as we looked to move on with a draw. At 75–5, it wasn't really working out for us and yours truly had to play a rather uncharacteristically patient innings to put us on an even keel. The only way there was going to be a result was if we'd failed to reach the follow-on, but that was saved and from there the draw was certain.

Up to Manchester and a Test match we simply had to win. Defeat meant the Ashes were lost and no one wanted to cough them up quite so early. However, I must admit that that was the most disjointed side I had been in for a long time and confidence was practically at rock bottom. Lubo wore the expression of a captain on his last legs throughout that summer and in Manchester he had very little left to give – not that it was going to stop him trying his heart out. We'd had terrible luck with injuries, with the likes of Graham Dilley, Robin Smith, Allan Lamb and Neil Foster all being ruled out at one stage or another, while Mike Gatting's mother-in-law suddenly passed away, leaving him out of the equation, before the issue of the rebel tour to South Africa reared its head.

That was something that had been lurking in the background throughout that summer and it wasn't helping things, much in the same way the Packer situation had destabilised the Aussies in the late 1970s. I was offered a huge sum of money to turn my back on England and join the rebel tour, but in the end I couldn't do it. The money would have been nice, but that is not the be-all and end-all; besides, I wasn't exactly on the breadline. It was more to do with the principle of it and what I wanted to achieve as a cricketer. I had done a lot by then already, but the back injury and the twenty-three months I'd had out of the England side meant that I still wanted to do more with the three lions on my shirt. I've said it before, but when you're going through hours of painful and lonely rehab, you do it because you want to win games for your country again. You want to enjoy the feeling of having a full house cheering you on again, and that is what pushes you to get fit.

If I had accepted the money to go to South Africa, I would never have got that again. As it was, the reassurances I thought I had from the likes of Micky Stewart were not upheld, and in many ways my efforts proved to be in vain – although I wasn't to know that at this stage.

What I did know was that England were about to lose the Ashes in as meek and feeble a way as I had ever known. We simply had to put up a fight, but at Old Trafford the lack of confidence was there for all to see. Only Robin Smith could claim to have done what was asked of him, while the rest of us were guilty as sin. Personally, I had a plan when I went in at 132–4, but it didn't work out at all as I had hoped. In much the same way as I had done in 1981, I felt that on day one, with so much time left in the game, the best form of defence was a counter-attacking punch. There was little point in hanging around going nowhere before getting out; you had to score runs while you were at the wicket. In my haste to get that counter-attack going, I picked the wrong ball from Trevor Hohns to hit and was bowled going for an almighty blow. I realise it didn't look very good, but those are the margins you deal with, and if it had come off, who knows what might have happened. We were bowled out for 260 and in reply the Aussies nudged their way to 219–3 by day two. They were in the driving seat on this trip, as per usual, but there would be a chink of light if day three went our way. It didn't.

No Australian batsman scored a century, so perhaps we could take some confidence from that. The only problem was that three of the buggers got more than eighty! It was the usual suspects, too: Taylor, Border and Waugh all enjoyed themselves, while Deano Jones cracked 69 for good measure.

At least the fourth day provided a chance to bat again and show some backbone in the face of all this Aussie pressure – only we didn't. We lost our top six inside 23 overs for 59 runs, and it was only a stand of 64 between Jack Russell and John Emburey that saved us from being beaten inside four days.

That night, as I made my way back to the hotel knowing the Ashes were as good as gone and there was very little I could do about it, I felt a sudden wave of anger wash over me. There were issues that had gone against us, for sure, like the injuries and the rebel tour rumours, but what annoyed me more than anything else was that I didn't feel we had given a proper account of ourselves throughout the series. We could and should have been much harder to beat, but instead of making the Aussies' lives a misery, we let them walk all over us, and that upset me. I know the guys in the team throughout the series had given their absolute best, but it wasn't good enough, and that is a rough old sting to take.

Still, we had to turn up again the following morning and by then my mood had lightened only a touch. What brought me back into the plus side was the sight of Jack Russell reaching his maiden Test ton against the old enemy. He displayed some guts and determination that day, not only frustrating and thwarting the Aussies but showing people at home that he was a capable batsman too. He was a magical gloveman, the closest we've had to Alan Knott, I feel, and here he was doing his bit with the bat too. It was great stuff. Once John Emburey had gone for 64, though, there wasn't quite enough in the tail to get the lead past 100. Terry Alderman got another five-fer, leaving the Aussies more than enough time to score the 81 they needed. With it came a nine-wicket win and the Ashes, with two games left to go.

The Australian win was well deserved, that much was clear. They had done almost everything better than us and they had also done it when it mattered, so you had to take your hat off to them. They were tough and uncompromising, which is how Test cricket should be played, and we were found wanting.

On the day they sealed the win, though, their thunder was stolen by the news that 16 Englishmen would be undertaking a rebel tour to South Africa under the stewardship of Mike Gatting the following winter. It was an uncomfortable situation that had distracted many a player and now the tour had become the main news on a day when Ashes cricket should have been front and centre, even though we had lost. All the talk was about how long each of the rebel players would be banned for and how their careers would be ruined for ever. It is with a wry smile that you can look back on all of that, knowing how things turned out. The likes of Gatt and Goochie, who had led the first rebel tour in 1982, not only went on to play much more cricket for England but are now well-established men within the game, paid by the England and Wales Cricket Board to work as cricket partnerships manager and batting coach respectively. No one would have thought that would be possible back in 1989.

All the furore over that tour slightly overshadowed the fact that England had coughed up the Ashes in double-quick time and now had two Test matches in which to salvage a bit of pride.

What happened next has to be considered not only the lowest point in my Ashes career but the lowest point in English Ashes cricket bar the two 5–0 results suffered in 2006–07 and 1920–21.

We went to Nottingham for the fifth Test with a new-look side that included a certain Mike Atherton, later my co-

commentator, who became a teammate of mine at the age of 21. He was so fresh-faced when he joined the dressing-room, very quiet and unassuming, but already with a steeliness that would prop up English cricket for a decade. He was picked for his sound technique and on the recommendations of trusted cricket men who thought they had seen something special in him. His first-class career wasn't that impressive on numbers alone, but, as he went on to prove, statistics aren't everything. He would have to wait for his chance to bat, however, as our summer took yet another nosedive, if such a thing was even possible by that stage.

Geoff Marsh and Mark Taylor opened the batting on day one and were still there as we all trudged off 102 overs, 301 runs and zero wickets later. For Taylor, it really was business as usual, but for Marsh, who hadn't scored a fifty before this knock, it was a bit of a surprise – the extra kick in the teeth our boys didn't need. It was a gorgeous day for batting, the sort of day that makes you wonder why you ever decided to be a bowler, but still, to not take a single wicket was heartbreaking. The following morning, the pair had registered the highest-ever Ashes opening partnership in history when Marsh gave me a catch at slip. We were really into them now!

To be fair, I do recall us bowling with a lot more discipline on day two, but it was still a case of damage limitation. Taylor's double ton helped take them to 560–5 by the close, with Gus Fraser bowling an immaculate line and length, which was to be the hallmark of his career. That day, though, was a bad one for me. I dived to my right to try to cling on to a lightning edge by David Boon off the bowling of Devon Malcolm. We all knew that Devon was quick, if a little erratic, but I found out just how quick when I got a finger to the ball; it was bent back in an instant and was dislocated. The pain was excruciating, but it only really felt as bad as my mood at our situation in the match.

With 602 runs on the board the Aussies had us in trouble. But when Terry Alderman again ran through us to take 5–69, we had waved goodbye to trouble and walked head first into a fiery pit. Robin Smith was the only plus point for us again, taking on Merv Hughes in a classic contest that he most definitely got the better of. Hughes had given Smith a barrage in the Lord's Test earlier in the summer when he ran down the pitch after beating the bat and snarled, 'You can't f***ing bat!' Judgey took it in his stride and hammered the next ball for four, after which he smartly told big Merv, 'Hey, we make a fine pair, don't we? I can't f***ing bat and you can't f***ing bowl!'

This time, it was all Judge as he hit the Aussies all over the park in lone defiance of our situation. I couldn't bat until number 9 in the order due to my finger, but I hung around for an hour making a painful and painfully slow 12. We had next to no chance of saving the follow-on, so the fourth day was all about creeping up somewhere near the Aussie total and giving ourselves a chance of saving the game. Getting bowled out for 117 and losing by an innings and 180 runs said it all. The heaviest defeat the Aussies had ever inflicted on us in England was hard to take, but by that stage it wasn't exactly a surprise.

Lubo was as depressed as I've ever known him and there was little anyone could do to cheer him up. We travel around the world commentating these days and he is permanently jolly. He has such a sunny disposition that it seems strange now to think that he was ever that low, but that is what a 4–0 scoreline in the Ashes can to do you when you've still got one left to play.

It had been a frustrating summer for me. I had had my moments, but I didn't exert the same hold over Australia as I once did. It was clear that AB would not give me the satisfaction of enjoying myself in these contests as I had done in the past. There was very little of the usual chat between the sides on the field. If anything, the Aussies were just ruthless in their approach and they had a group of young players who clearly enjoyed that part of the fight. They gave nothing away all summer, whereas we had given away everything. My finger injury meant that I couldn't play at the Oval, although I made myself available for the West Indies tour that followed, going back on a decision not to tour any more. The anger I felt at losing the Ashes had left me with a desire to do something more for England and success against the Windies would have come close to dealing with that.

At least England would be going on tour with a crumb of comfort after managing to avoid defeat in the sixth and final Test of the summer. From a distance, though, it was clear that the issues afflicting us throughout the series were still there at the death, and only darkened skies on the final day meant a 5–0 scoreline was avoided. Yet again Australia's first innings climbed above 450 and yet again Mark Taylor was in the runs, the only surprise being that he didn't get to his hundred. That honour was reserved for Dean Jones.

Half-centuries from Lubo and Gladstone Small avoided the follow-on and certain defeat, although AB's decision to give his bowlers just four hours to win the match nearly paid off, and that would really have been the final straw. In the end, a punchy 77 not out from the Judge was enough to share the honours in that match, so 4–0 was the final score.

Ted Dexter's bizarre claim 'I am not aware of any mistakes that I've made' only served to make the point that he had been wandering around in his own little world for the duration of the summer. I realise we had a lot of injury problems right throughout the series, but to use 29 players is a bit steep in anyone's books.

The Ashes had gone and English cricket was feeling very low indeed. No one was to know, though, that the next decade would be even worse. As far as the Ashes was concerned, this was the beginning of a period of total dominance that was hard to believe and even harder to swallow.

FANTASY TEAM 4

SPIN AND STRIKE BOWLERS

DEREK UNDERWOOD

I've not seen a better English spin bowler operate more consistently than Deadly Derek in my lifetime, and I've never seen a bloke look more tired and satisfied to get his feet up in the pavilion whether he had bowled five or twenty-five overs.

He was happiest at the end of a day's play in the dressing-room with a fag and a beer in his hands and he would continue into the night if given half the chance. That was why we got on so well, because more often than not he and I would be the last men standing in the hotel bars around the world as others would try to keep pace with us. Well, actually, Deadly was usually keen to get to his room, but I found I could persuade him to stay with a headlock! After one particularly boozy few days in India when he was trying to get a book written with Chris Lander, he vowed never to share a room with me again because it had all been a bit too much for him.

He would be brilliant in this team alongside a four-pronged pace attack, offering subtle changes of pace and teasing the batsmen as he went along.

Although second slip was my usual home in the field, I actually used to operate at silly point for Deadly most of the time. I was a young lad making my way when he was in the team and so that was where you were sent to field, but I didn't mind it at all because I took a few catches for him there and there was very little chance of me being in danger, since he rarely dropped the ball short enough to be cut.

He was a master of control with the ball, putting it where he wanted at precisely the right pace to make life tricky for the batsmen.

A lot of people unfairly say that he was only effective on a 'sticky dog', or a wet wicket, when the uncovered pitch had seen a bit of rain, but that wasn't true. He was perhaps most effective in those conditions, but he was pretty handy in others too. That is why he has still taken more wickets than any other English spinner.

There have been pretenders to his throne, like Phil Tufnell, John Emburey, Robert Croft, Ashley Giles and more recently Monty Panesar, but none has quite lasted the distance. Graeme Swann will fancy his chances of getting somewhere near Deadly after the year he's had, but it will be tougher than he thinks.

The brilliance of Deadly stemmed from his control of pace and flight and the angle of his delivery, because he wasn't a prodigious turner of the ball, he just did enough. I think the closest example to him in the current game is Daniel Vettori, who has complete mastery of what he is doing with the ball.

UNDERWOOD V. AUSTRALIA

Played: 29
Won: 8
Drew: 12
Lost: 9
Runs: 371
Average: 12.79
Wickets: 105
Average: 26.38
Five-fers: 4
Ashes won: 1970–71, 1977

BOB WILLIS

Even if I didn't know Bob the way I do, and even if I hadn't actually been there on the field, he would be an automatic pick for this team based purely on what he did at Headingley in 1981. When someone can do that for a team and turn a lost cause into the greatest Test win any of us are ever likely to see, they get a big tick next to their name. I still can't accept that they only gave one man-of-the-match prize in that game. Yes, I scored a few runs and gave us something to bowl at, but Australia should never have lost that match and if it hadn't been for Bob, they wouldn't have done.

He got himself into a zone that he had never been in before and hasn't been in since and created history, which I believe is what Ashes cricket can do to you. There have been so many crazy moments in this old contest that nothing should surprise us, but on that day Bob did something extraordinary. And let's not forget that Bob was lucky to be playing at all. He had been struggling with flu and was almost left out because of it. We've spoken about it since and Bob admits that had there not been a change of heart at the eleventh hour, he might never have played cricket for England again, and the history books would be completely different. He had dodgy knees, which needed serious surgery, and it was remarkable in itself that he managed to play as much as he did.

He did milk it a bit at times, though, and I can remember him deserting me at Sydney on the 1978–79 tour when it got a bit too hot for him and he went and sat in the shower for the rest of the day while I slogged my guts out getting through about three shirts in the day. He tried to make it up to me by dragging me out to some jazz club to listen to his funky music. To be fair, the band was good, but I wasn't about to tell him that. I always associate Bob with music because he is just so passionate about it. If he's not at a concert or a live gig, he's blaring it out in his room, and it's most likely to be his hero Bob Dylan.

Bob was as fearsome a strike bowler as you could want, all arms and legs, thundering in and getting more out of a pitch than anyone else. His height, and therefore bounce, was what made him so dangerous, and it's what gets good batsmen out. It is a weapon that every captain would love to have at his disposal, but, with the exception of the West Indies during the 1970s, these kind of bowlers don't grow on trees, and I just think we were lucky to have Bob when we did.

WILLIS V. AUSTRALIA

Played: 35
Won: 14
Drew: 9
Lost: 12
Runs: 383
Average: 10.35
Wickets: 128
Average: 26.14
Five-fers: 7
Ashes won: 1970–71, 1977, 1978–79, 1981

JOHN SNOW

A lot of people might find it odd that a man who writes poetry has made it into my fantasy XI, but John Snow was poetry in motion. He was absolutely effortless as he came in to bowl, and he generated great pace from such an easy action. The two volumes of poetry that he wrote as a player might not be part of my reading material on tour these days, but they are part and parcel of Snowy the individual whom I like.

He was a hard-headed and strong-willed cricketer and that is why he didn't play more than 49 Test matches for England; he was regularly being 'disciplined'. But anyone who stands up to the Establishment is all right in my book. He was dropped from his county side for apparently 'not trying', but, having faced him a few times, I'd hate to have been in the firing line when he was trying. I never actually played Test cricket with John Snow – my debut came one year after his last match – but I saw enough of him in county championship cricket over four years between 1974 and 1977 to know how good a bowler he was.

I also looked up to him for his feats against the Aussies, and in particular on the 1970–71 Illingworth tour, during which he took 31 wickets and was the ultimate spearhead, causing a bit of aggro after hitting Terry Jenner on the head with a bouncer, which a few punters didn't like at all. They threw beer cans at Snowy on the pitch, which was a disgrace, as was the fan who grabbed him by the shirt and tried to remonstrate with him. How he didn't turn round and lamp the idiot is beyond me. As it turned out, he ended up in hospital himself a little later when he broke his finger on the boundary fence trying to catch a six. While he was being operated on, the rest of the side did him proud by winning the game, giving him a great celebration to return to.

The anger stirred up by his short and fast bowling stemmed, I suspect, from lingering raw feelings about the Bodyline series, but it is funny how there wasn't any anger from the Aussies when Jeff Thomson was laying batsmen out all over the place four years later! Every successful cricket team has at least one fast, aggressive and ruthless bowling spearhead, and John Snow was the main weapon in England's armoury for much of the 1970s. This kind of cricketer is rare and should be looked after, but the authorities in those days wanted everyone to toe the party line and do as they were told, regardless of how ridiculous it all was. Snowy would be treasured in my fantasy team, as long as he kept his poetry recitals to a bare minimum – like never.

SNOW V. AUSTRALIA

Played: 20
Won: 5
Drew: 11
Lost: 4
Runs: 392
Average: 15.07
Wickets: 83
Average: 25.61
Five-fers: 4
Ashes won: 1970–71

SHANE WARNE

Simply the greatest cricketer of my lifetime and arguably the greatest ever. The reason is that he single-handedly put cricket back on the map. He made cricket sexy again when it was threatening to die. He got people interested. All this and he did it with leg-spin! It should have been a fast bowler or a flashing batsman; I mean, who ever thought leg-spin was worth a moment's thought until Warney came along? In an instant, every kid wanted to bowl like him and be like him. He was flamboyant and free-spirited, he had his own unique blond and zinced-up look, but at the centre of it all was his ability to play cricket.

I never played international cricket with Warney and I can only remember playing against him a couple of times in 1993 in tour matches, but I have seen more than enough over the years to form my opinion of him, and it is a pretty good one.

Let's take his bowling first of all. He changed the role of a spinner in the game of cricket, thanks to his variations, his mastery of the art and above all his control. He allowed Allan Border, Mark Taylor, Steve Waugh and Ricky Ponting to use him as an attacking bowler, a stock bowler, a strike bowler and an 'if all else fails' bowler. With Warne in the side, you were never out of a game, because to begin with he could spin batsmen out and then in later life he could scare batsmen out with the force of his personality. He made batsmen think that everything he did was part of an elaborate plan, so even when it wasn't he had already won the battle with the opposition. He had the variations to back it up, kidding guys with the flipper and the slider as well as the googly. The beauty of it was that sometimes it was just an ordinary ball, but he made you think it was something special. The number of conversations I've had over the years with England batsmen who just didn't know what to do against him would shock you.

His bowling was only part of his armoury, though, because he was smart with it. Always talking to the batsman, not being rude or overly aggressive, just making little comments that would get under the skin and eventually cause their downfall. He would talk to the umpires, telling them to watch out for things like his ball that went straight on, so he could get more lbw decisions.

Beyond all that, he just loved being out there. You could tell that there was no place he would rather be – except maybe at the MCG in an Aussie rules shirt, because that was his first love. He was the greatest captain Australia never had, but in a way I'm glad he didn't take the extra responsibility, because it wouldn't have allowed him to stay the same bloke he always has been. I first met Shane in 1995, filming a Nike advert based around his 'mystery ball' at the SCG in Sydney, and from the moment we shook hands a friendship began. He enjoys life like I do, he likes a beer and he likes his food, but he is always prepared to perform on the field. He didn't need a psychologist to get him ready for a game, he didn't need a fitness coach pushing him to do bleep test after bleep test, he just needed a ball and a field and he would do the rest.

One thing I should point out, though, is that his natural talent did not make him the bowler he is on its own. He worked bloody hard at his game as a youngster, bowling over after over after over until he knew exactly what he was doing with a cricket ball, and it is important to appreciate that. He may have been a bit of a joker on and off the field, but he knew when to be serious and his hard work paid off.

He dominated Ashes cricket for 14 years, until his retirement, and he saved his best till last. I know the 'Ball of the Century' was a special moment, but his 40 wickets in a losing cause in 2005 together with his spell at Adelaide that started the collapse in 2006 are two images of him that tell you everything you need to know. He's the ultimate competitor and a natural born winner. I haven't even mentioned his dangerous batting or his useful slip catching (or his disappointing golf), but in truth I don't think I need to.

WARNE v. ENGLAND

> Played: 36
> Won: 24
> Drew: 5
> Lost: 7
> Runs: 946
> Average: 22.00
> Wickets: 195
> Average: 23.25
> Five-fers: 11
> Ashes won: 1993, 1994–95, 1997, 1998–99, 2001, 2002–03, 2006–07

JEFF THOMSON

If there was a bowler who gave batsmen sleepless nights about facing him in the morning, it was Thommo. In a quiet moment, Viv Richards once told me that Thommo was the fastest bowler he had ever faced in the game, and this is a guy who grew up being tested by the most incredible battery of fast bowlers in practice almost every day. And when he was West Indies captain, he was facing guys striving to get into the team, desperate to prove to him how good they were. But, for him, Thommo was still the quickest.

That will do for me, because the honest truth is that I never got to face him at his quickest and I consider myself very lucky. On the 1974–75 tour to Australia, he was unleashed on England's batsmen and they came home battered and bruised. Although he was still quick enough when I played him in 1977 and 1982, he was a bit smarter rather than going for tearaway pace, thanks to a shoulder injury he picked up in an on-field collision with Alan Turner in 1976. His slingy, javelin-style action made him hard to pick up because you couldn't see the ball all the way from his hand. It would disappear behind his back and then you had to try to pick it up in the fraction of a second you had when he released it. That was what made him, and especially his bouncer, so tricky to play. Also, the fact that he did actually like hitting batsmen meant he would do whatever he could for his delivery to be a surprise.

Thommo is what I think of as an archetypal Aussie: a blond, beach-loving, beer-drinking, straight-talking larrikin. What you see is what you get. There was no mystery to Thommo; he just wanted to rough you up and spit you out – that was his idea of fun. He spends a fair amount of time in the UK and we get to meet up every now and then, and he is my most feared night out. Coming from me, that says a lot; I know I'm most people's most feared night out, so what does that make Thommo? The guy knows how to have a good time and he will keep going and going and going. Beer or wine, it makes no difference, because he has an iron constitution and even I have trouble keeping up.

THOMSON v. ENGLAND

> Played: 21
> Won: 8
> Drew: 7
> Lost: 6
> Runs: 295
> Average: 14.75
> Wickets: 100
> Average: 24.18
> Five-fers: 5
> Ashes won: 1974–75, 1975, 1982–83

GLENN MCGRATH

When a bowler like Glenn McGrath comes along, you thank your lucky stars and set about conquering the world.

Australia would not have dominated the game as they did if they had not had 'Pigeon' to lead their attack. They would have been pretty good with just Shane Warne, but with McGrath they went to another level. What is totally unfair is to say that he just bowled at the top of off-stump. People try to boil McGrath's career down to just line and length with a little bit of movement, and that was that – as if it was as easy as pie. McGrath was so much better than that and, as a bowler myself, I think watching him operate was a thing of beauty.

He might not have had the raw pace of the great West Indians or of a Lillee or Thomson, but he had unerring control of a cricket ball, and control means power. He was able to read a pitch better than any bowler I've seen, so if there was a bit more swing, he would pitch it up, and if there was a bit more movement, he would bring it back, and if there was neither, he would find the right line to stop whichever batsman he faced scoring runs. It is not easy to hit the top of off-stump, because a lot of batsmen practise hitting balls from there; he needed to get it just right for his opponent, at the right pace and angle to make it work, and that was what he was good at.

When he got onto a surface and a ground that he loved, like Lord's, he was virtually unplayable, as England found out in 1997, 2001 and 2005, when he wrote his name on the honours board each time. If he'd been fit in 2005, he might not have prevented England winning the Ashes, but the reaction in the home dressing-room when they saw his name missing from the team sheet was unbridled joy. It was no coincidence that the two games he missed due to his ankle injury were the two games England won.

He did give cricket watchers some very funny moments, too, whenever he went out to bat, because he literally couldn't do it, no matter how hard he tried. But under Steve Waugh he did actually learn how to keep the ball out, if not how to score runs, and the fact that he managed to help save the draw at Old Trafford in 2005 remains one of his proudest achievements.

He was also a very tough cookie, especially in his younger days, when he would have a few choice words to say to the batsman, in the great tradition of Aussie fast bowlers. His run-in with Ramnaresh Sarwan almost spilled over the top, and if I were Sarwan, I'd be glad it didn't. McGrath is an old country farming boy and the sort of tools he uses in day-to-day life are pretty sharp. In fact, Allan Border told me a funny story about him, that on his first few tours while all the other boys were getting ready for a couple of months away with the odd purchase of *Penthouse* or *Playboy*, Pigeon was busy buying *Guns and Ammo*! AB said, 'I was very worried about him to begin with, but he reassured me that was what country boys were into. When the rooms were being divvied up at the team hotel, Glenn did usually get a room to himself, though.'

Pigeon has been king of the fast bowlers for much of his career and scotches the theory that you have to have raw pace to be able to take Test wickets. What also sets him apart is the way that he triumphed on the cricket field while also supporting his late wife, Jane, in her battle with breast cancer. He is a devoted family man who excelled on and off the pitch. I can't imagine what it must have been like for him to lose his wife, but the way he has thrown himself into charitable work on behalf of her and the McGrath Foundation has been nothing short of heroic, and I wish him all the best in the world with it. A true cricketing icon.

FANTASY TEAM 4

McGrath v. England

Played: 30
Won: 22
Drew: 4
Lost: 4
Runs: 105
Average: 6.17
Wickets: 157
Average: 20.92
Five-fers: 10
Ashes won: 1994–95, 1997, 1998–99, 2001, 2002–03, 2006–07

COMING TO A CLOSE

By 1990, my body was constantly arguing with me over what I wanted it to do. If I needed it to pound in on the softer early-season ground, my knee went. If I wanted it to prove a point on the harder late-season ground, my hamstring went. I couldn't really win, and at the same time I was distinctly out of favour with England. It was Goochie's side and he wanted to find the next all-rounder whom England could count on, but as it turned out finding another Botham was trickier than people thought.

My injuries stopped me from heading to Australia for the 1990–91 tour, and although I was happy enough doing a spot of panto back at home, I yearned to be out there sticking it to the Aussies once more. The truth was, though, I'm not sure how much of an impact I would have made. When you're spending so much time on the sidelines, it is difficult to get into any kind of rhythm for Test cricket – and unless I could get myself physically sorted, I wouldn't get any more of that, full stop.

While I was doing my best wooden-plank impression in *Jack and the Beanstalk*, Goochie and the boys were getting a humping on what turned out to be quite a miserable tour, from what I gather. David Gower's Tiger Moth episode might not have been to everyone's taste, but it was the only high point of that trip. However, the fallout from that little adventure highlighted what a miserable place the England camp was around this time.

I was out of it, but I heard a few things from players when they got back and it just sounded like the relentless, hard-working regime of Goochie was a bit counterproductive. In addition, I think it is fair to say that the quality of English cricketers around the time had taken a bit of a dip. The effort and enthusiasm were still there, but they couldn't quite match up to the Australian product and that was to continue for years yet.

In Queensland, Lubo and John Morris tried to pick spirits up at a stage when England had already lost the Ashes and were trying to play for some pride. In Carrara, they had both already batted and decided to take advantage of a local service that took visitors up in 1938 Tiger Moths. Lubo actually asked tour manager Peter Lush for the money to go up in the planes and he gladly handed it over, not knowing what it was for, of course. When they were up and buzzing over the ground, Robin Smith reached his century out in the middle, so they flew in closer and tighter, much to the Judge's amusement. He gave them a salute and they gave one back to him. It was a bit of light-hearted fun, but, as they should have known by then, you can only really have fun if you're winning, and England certainly weren't. They were 2–0 down in the series, thanks to defeats at Brisbane and Melbourne, so the management looked on the stunt very unfavourably indeed. Lubo told them they could come down hard on him or just look on it as a prank; the £1,000 fine that followed told him what they thought of it, and the accompanying statement that declared it to be 'immature, ill-judged and ill-timed' wasn't exactly what he'd hoped for.

It seemed to me that, as great a batsman, cricketer and tactical captain as Goochie was, his man-management methods stifled the life out of many a cricketer. Lubo was the greatest batsman of his generation and should have been given a bit more freedom, as well as being given a bit more support by those in charge. Towards the end of his England career, despite having given the Aussies what for as a batsman and as a captain for years, he was treated like a youngster coming into a county side rather than the great that he was, and I couldn't stand it. In many ways, it was a good thing I wasn't around the group at that stage because Goochie would certainly have known my feelings on it.

In fact, I did make it perfectly clear what I thought about things at the 1992 World Cup, when we were the best team there but were flogged to death by his fitness-fanatic regime and ultimately we were a tired bunch in the final. By the sound of things, the boys out in Australia had done a lot of fitness training as well, yet they still got spanked, so the theory that more running and sweating off the field makes for a better team on it is not quite true. Also, the lesson to be learned from the previous tour in 1986–87 was that there was a time and a place for real hard work and that was usually in the Test matches, but with Gatt off leading his rebel tour that message didn't make it through, or at least it fell on deaf ears. The rebel tour itself naturally removed a fair few players from selection and there were some injury problems for England too, but there is little question that the Australians had the better team that time, and they proved it.

The 1993 season was always going to be my last. My body was hurting whether I had bowled 15 overs the day before or not and it was proving to be tough just getting out of bed. But how can you turn your back on the chance to play Australia when they have provided so many moments of unbridled joy and dark despair in your life? It is oxygen to someone like me, and I just had to have one more crack. I would probably still get my whites on to play the Aussies today if they fitted me!

So even though I had played only a minor part the previous summer and was clearly out of favour with England, I really thought I could stick it to Border's boys again. AB was lording it up with two successive Ashes wins over the Poms and, to be fair to him, he was reaping the rewards of some serious work behind the scenes, and it made up for some shocking years in the mid-1980s.

England had lost the last two Ashes contests 4–0 and 3–0, so anything involving at least one win in England's column would have been an improvement. The fact was, though, that AB had a fine team with him. The Waugh twins, Mark Taylor and David Boon were a useful batting line-up, while Craig McDermott was a spearhead to rival any in the world and Merv Hughes had matured into a quality fast bowler. But let's not kid ourselves here: 1993 would only really be remembered for the Ashes debut of one Shane Keith Warne.

Who was to know that this bleached-blond, pizza-and-chips-chomping, larrikin Aussie rules wannabe would actually be the greatest spin bowler ever to play Ashes cricket? Certainly not me.

I was up in Durham playing with one of the best middle-order batsmen Australia had had in recent years in the shape of Dean Jones, who didn't make the tour party, and when I asked him about the various players they were bringing over he didn't sound that impressed. Maybe there was a bit of the macho 'not as good as me' in what he was saying, but Deano has always been an honest assessor of what he sees and he just didn't seem to think that Australian vintage would be as tough to beat as the last, largely because he felt the bowling lacked a bit of a spark.

He had heard some good things about Warne, and he did say to watch out for the leggie when he gave it a rip, because few blokes spun it that far, but apart from that I wasn't expecting a world-beater to emerge there and then.

But that is the thing with great players. They don't need an invitation to grab a game by the scruff of the neck; they just do it. They don't wait until they are allowed to steal the headlines; they just do it. And that was the case with Warney.

I first caught sight of him in the early-season warm-up when I was asked to play in the traditional tour-opener Duchess of Norfolk match at Arundel. If I'm honest, though, the last person I was thinking about on that day was Shane Warne. For me, it was a chance to prove that I could still mix it with the big boys and that I could still offer some kind of advantage over the Australians. They knew it and I knew it: when it came to Botham v. Australia, things went up a notch, and they didn't quite know what I would produce. As it turned out, I had a decent day, taking 2–29 from my 10 overs.

What followed, though, was a disgrace as far as I'm concerned. I silenced the clever dick who, after I'd been hit for four, shouted, 'It's 1993 now, not 1981!' by getting the wickets of Damien Martyn, who we all know is a top-class batsman, and my old chum AB, who simply hated getting out to me because he knew it would come up in conversation the next few times I saw him. Yet when quizzed about my performance after the game, chairman of selectors Ted Dexter scoffed at the scalps and asked the radio interviewer, 'What were they trying to do? Get Ian back into the England side?' I was seething. How could he think that any Australian would ever give his wicket away and why would he do it to help a Pom like me?! It was ludicrous and, regardless of whether it meant I wouldn't play for England again, I wanted an apology, because it was downright rude of him to cast those kinds of aspersions. I got my apology in the end, but the whole episode was brushed under the carpet.

As far as Warney went, he took no wickets in the game, but for a leg-spinner he bowled quite tightly. That turned out to be a huge feature of his game and one reason why he went on to be so successful. If he wasn't taking wickets, he wasn't going for many runs either, and that in itself built up pressure, which leads to more wickets. I didn't get any sense of the drama Warney would unleash on the rest of that summer, though. He actually seemed reasonably quiet, which is a strange thing to say because those of you who've ever met Shane will know he is exactly like his persona on the field. He is the life and soul of any room and now that he joins the commentary team at Sky on occasions, he makes the place even more fun than before.

The first Test was at Old Trafford and I was nowhere near the England side, so I resigned myself to catching bits and pieces when I could and concentrated on doing what I could for Durham.

I was never a great watcher of cricket while I was playing. The days when I would sit and watch matches at Lord's as part of the groundstaff were long gone. I always found playing so much more enjoyable than watching, and so, even though the Ashes were on, I didn't make a beeline for the TV – until one particular delivery.

I have to be honest and own up to the fact that I didn't actually watch Warney's Ball of the Century live because I was too busy trying to bowl my own for Durham against Leicestershire at Grace Road. We were in the field when Warney came on to bowl and when he managed to turn one from a foot outside leg-stump to hit off-stump, we thought someone had done themselves a mischief. The noise and kerfuffle coming from the pavilion and various rooms around the ground with TVs was so unusual we knew something had happened, but we just didn't know what.

It was only when we'd got off the field for tea that we were able to watch a replay, and I couldn't believe my eyes. How a cricket ball was able to turn past the width of Mike Gatting and still hit the stumps was quite incredible. The comedy line often trotted out now is that had it been a pork pie, Gatt would definitely have got it. But the ball spun so sharply and with such drift, it was just impossible to do anything other than walk back to the pavilion.

I used to enjoy facing spinners when I was playing and I've often told Warney that he was lucky he didn't deliver that first ball to me, because it would have gone the distance, to which he replies, 'You'd have gone the distance back to the dressing-room, Beef!' Well, he did have his chance to get me out at Arundel and didn't take it, so he's never going to win that argument. Warney stole the headlines that day and it was obvious to see why, but I can think of one man who wouldn't have been too pleased with that. England's own spinner Peter Such had actually enjoyed a pretty good time of it himself, grabbing 6–67 on debut, but no one was interested. Poor old Suchy. At least he can be happy in the knowledge that he was outshone by the greatest spinner ever to play the game.

Australia won that match comfortably before moving on to Lord's for an even more straightforward win, by an innings. The Aussie batsmen came within one run of their entire top four getting centuries, but thankfully Phil Tufnell bowled Mark Waugh on 99 to salvage some pride, although, at 452–3, I'm not sure what pride there was to save!

Things didn't exactly get much better from there, although the emergence of Graham Thorpe to score a hundred on debut in the second innings at Trent Bridge was a rare highlight as we managed to secure a draw.

With England losing 2–0 with three to play, there was just an outside chance that the selectors might turn to me in the desperate hope of igniting some kind of turnaround that would confound all the evidence before them. It was therefore not a total surprise when Ted Dexter called me at home one evening. I should have known to expect the unexpected where Ted was concerned, though. The team he asked me to play for was not the one gifting the Ashes to the Aussies but one that was about to take on Holland in Amsterdam. He asked me to captain the England A side. I gave him short shrift and moved on.

In fact, soon after that conversation I moved on for good. I spotted a little gem of a game in the fixture list: Durham v. Australia just before the fourth Test of the summer. Immediately, I knew it would be my last game of cricket as a professional.

No sooner had I made that decision than I felt a huge weight had been lifted from my shoulders. Not because I was under any great pressure at that stage, but it meant that my life would be hugely different and the game that had given me everything would no longer fill my thoughts nine to five. I didn't really know what I would do with myself after quitting, but I was satisfied that I had done everything I could have done while I had the chance, and that was enough for me.

Getting the opportunity to finish against Australia was a huge thrill because the Aussies had provided a constant backdrop to my life. The biggest highs and most crushing lows had resulted from Ashes campaigns and had shaped my life for better or worse.

I told Kath and the necessary people at Durham that my career was coming to a close, and there was the obvious attention on me and the game, with my valedictory press conference lasting almost an hour, but on that occasion I didn't mind chatting with the press, giving them chapter and verse – having given my old mate Chris Lander from the *Daily Mirror* the exclusive first.

We cracked on with the game at the Racecourse Ground, a beautiful setting if ever there was one, with Durham Cathedral rising magnificently behind one end. It was a fitting place to bring my career to a close. I hit 32 in my last-ever innings before Brendon Julian caught me off the bowling of Steve Waugh. There were a few lusty blows in there just to remind the Aussies that they would never have everything their own way against me, but unfortunately I went for one shot too many and got out. At the time, no one knew it would be my last innings, but, thanks to

Simon Brown's 7–70 with the ball, the Aussies had to follow on.

There was a bit of rain around and with Matthew Hayden and David Boon batting particularly well the game petered out into a draw. Not before I'd bowled my last over, though, and for Boonie it was probably one he'd want to forget.

He had been enjoying a glorious tour, scoring centuries in the previous two Test matches as well as a 93 at Old Trafford, but Boonie was a bit of a worrier, and on that tour 21 year olds Hayden and Damien Martyn were scoring runs for fun in the county games and putting pressure on everyone in the top order. He had nothing to worry about, really, but as I came in to bowl my last-ever ball as a professional, I couldn't resist giving him a real test. I took my fella out of my trousers and came charging in to bowl. First of all, Boonie wasn't laughing. He stopped me and refused to face up to the ball(s). But with a wink and a smile, I soon had him seeing the funny side and by the time I got to the wicket he was in stitches 'No, Beefy, you can't do this to me!' I did, and we both came through it unscathed. He went on to make another century on the tour, while I took my cap and sweater and told skipper David Graveney that I was done.

When the game finished, I was given a heartfelt congratulatory handshake by both Steve Waugh and Matthew Hayden, the senior pro and the young tiger, which was nice. The fact that both men have now retired after scoring about a zillion runs for Australia really shows my age. I said my bit to the Durham dressing-room and then went and had a beer with the Aussies in theirs, as I had always done over the years. I can't really remember a time when I didn't have a beer with the Aussies after play and that is part of what makes competing against them so special. You will go hammer and tongs trying to beat each other on the field and then when it is all said and done you're friends again and you can share a drink together. I haven't been able to do that with every team that I've played against, but with the Aussies that was certainly the case. We should never, ever lose sight of that. The day an England cricketer can't go and say 'well played' to his Aussie opposition or vice versa will be the day that cricket has died.

While I was in the Aussie changing-room in Durham, I was having a good chat about what was going on in the current series and none of them could believe how easily England were rolling over. Guys like Boonie and AB, who wasn't playing but was keeping an eye on things, were telling me that this wasn't the England they were used to playing and they knew already with three Tests to go that they would go close to winning all three. They were right about that.

Throughout that summer of 1993, I felt like things were coming to a natural end for me, and for England things were going from bad to worse. Warney immediately had the wood over our batsmen, which was to continue for the next 13 years, while their batsmen, led by the likes of Slater and Waugh, were gorging themselves on runs galore. However, it is only fair that I pay due respect to a bloke who really made himself into a hero on that trip and the bloke I had a few beers with after my final match – Merv Hughes.

Merv and I had a bit of history, going back to when I hit him for 22 in one over in 1986. I liked him, but I also thought the way he carried on with the sledging and tough-guy attitude was a lot of bluster and bravado without much to back it up. He had forged a decent enough set of stats as an Australian paceman alongside Craig McDermott, but I just hadn't seen anything that really impressed me until 1993.

He was no spring chicken either by that stage and his body had started to creak too. He was always a big bloke and I knew how hard it can be to keep the weight down when injury prevents you from playing as much as you want to. But on that trip, he was tremendous, and the Ashes would not have made their way back to Australia had it not been for his 31 wickets. What impressed me most was the way he carried the Australian pace attack on his shoulders in the absence of McDermott.

During the Lord's Test, the Aussie firebrand was found bent over in the foetal position in the showers during their first innings with most of his teammates thinking he'd had a dodgy prawn at lunch. As it turned out, he had a twisted bowel and had to go straight home to get it sorted out. That left big Merv and youngster Julian to carry the pace burden, and Merv was a colossus. He tore in at the England batsmen both with the ball and with his tongue, and all this while he was suffering with a chronic knee injury. His knee had locked up at various times during the tour and after the third Test his groin had gone too, but he never quit, and that showed a bloke with real ticker, which is what you expect from an Aussie cricketer.

He didn't play in Durham but he was up there with the rest of the squad and it was during that game that Steve Waugh actually found the diet diary that he was keeping. Merv had been using a dietician of his own who'd told him to keep a diary of everything he ate, and Waugh read out one of the entries from a day in London when he had gone to Planet Hollywood. It read: 'Had bowl of nachos, a dozen chicken wings, a chicken burger, half a chicken burger that someone couldn't finish, a chocolate dessert, 15 pints of lager, a Beetlejuice cocktail, and a Terminator cocktail.' Yet this bloke, dubbed 'Sumo' by the English fans, kept charging in, taking wicket after wicket, and for that he must be respected. He was a player after my own heart with that kind of regime!

With all the chat about food, he told me a great story about his old Victorian mate Warney, who had been rooming with him in Adelaide the year before. The Aussie physio Errol Alcott used to monitor what the players had from room service by checking the trays outside their doors, so when Merv and Warney had polished off a plate of burgers and chips, the old bowler told his young mate to go and put the tray outside someone else's room. Warney happened to be naked when he was doing it and Merv couldn't waste an opportunity like that; he quickly sprang out of bed and locked him out. Poor old Warney had to bang on the door and beg his mate to let him back in, but every time he banged the door his crown jewels were on show and Merv reckons it took him a good ten minutes to find the key to unlock the door!

One thing is for sure, Merv managed to unlock the door to a stackful of England wickets on the 1993 tour, tormenting the likes of Graham Hick with the odd sledge that can't have been too funny or clever but worked.

With my career now at an end, I could see that Australia were building something with some very useful cricketers, but with Border, Boon, McDermott and Hughes unlikely to be around for much longer, I thought their dominance might only last at best another series. Of course, I hadn't really heard of Glenn McGrath, Adam Gilchrist, Justin Langer or Jason Gillespie at that stage.

The series moved on to Headingley, where Boonie had recovered sufficiently from our previous engagement to score a brilliant hundred, while Border and Waugh collected a double ton and ton respectively so they could declare on a whopping 653–4. England's 200 all out in reply as Paul Reiffel, now a respected umpire, and Merv ripped through the line-up was just pathetic. There were clearly some tired bodies and minds in the England camp, but this was just abject, with no man scoring more than 59. Following on, the same men did the damage, with off-spinner Tim May getting in on the act too as England officially lost the Ashes thanks to an innings and 148-run defeat. It was a humping whichever way you wanted to carve it up, and things had to change.

Goochie realised that his days of leading the three lions were over. He had been a loyal servant to the game and was as proud a captain as you are likely to find, but his methods were not getting the results he wanted and, after such a crushing blow, he knew his time was up. There would be more runs from him, of course, but he resigned the captaincy and moved aside to let the young Athers take over.

The immediate improvement England would have wanted didn't materialise at Edgbaston, though, as poor old Athers was taken to the cleaners by eight wickets. Paul Reiffel was again outstanding in taking a six-fer, but the real star of the show was Mark Waugh, who was the epitome of elegance in stroking 137, a contrast to both the blood and thunder of Slater and the dogged accumulation of his brother and AB. The Aussies just seemed to have every base covered and when one man failed to stand up, another just stood up in his place. That is how the best teams work and England had no answer.

When it came to the final Test at the Oval, I feared a 5–0 scoreline, but that was to come later. Perhaps it was tiredness on the Aussies' part or perhaps it was just a sign that the England boys had had enough of being flogged, but they came out fighting in London. There were fifties from Gooch, Atherton,

Hick and Stewart as England reached a decent 380 all out, which was a treat for them that summer. And with the ball, good old Gus Fraser did the damage.

I played with Angus on his debut in 1989 and he was a magnificent English seamer who rarely gave runs away unless they were earned, but he was a bit more skilful than just that. He could perform in all sorts of conditions. He took wickets in the Caribbean for fun and also Down Under, but a cruel hip injury when he was coming into his prime robbed him of a few years when his zip had him up with the quicker bowlers in the game. After that injury, it wasn't clear whether he would be able to cause problems for the very best batsmen, but at the Oval he showed he could still take wickets even though the express pace had gone. I like Gus a lot because he's a miserable so-and-so most of the time and then his face will just break out in a huge grin when something tickles his funny bone. He is an honest and hard-working cricket man who loves the game dearly, and I'm glad to see him in cricket administration now, because he won't take a lot of nonsense.

With a 77-run lead, England's batsmen dug deep for one last time in the series to leave the Aussies needing 391 to win. Mark Ramprakash's 64 was absolutely vital in that, and sadly it was one of the only too rare occasions that he fired for England. His record against Australia is actually not that bad, but it is one of life's great mysteries how he never managed to translate his total dominance of county attacks into international ones.

Australia had a day to survive and England had a day to bowl them out, and for the first time in 18 matches our boys won. It had been such a long time coming that even though the series had long gone, it still meant something special. In the years to come, the odd win here and there was all England were able to celebrate. But with a new young captain in charge and the career of Allan Border almost at an end, the 161-run win put enough cheer in English hearts to make people think the tide might be about to turn.

WATCHING THE SLUMP

When all is said and done, the things you hold on to most dearly are your memories. I had a truckload from my career as an England player, so when it came to the time for me to move on to the next phase in my life, I was able to do it without too much looking back.

I had a bit of time away from the game in the winter of 1993 and the summer of 1994, but made sure I was back in Australia for the Ashes tour the following winter. I wasn't a formal member of the Sky commentary box then, but discussions had taken place and it was clear I would be forging a second career during the next English season. Being out in Australia during the Ashes tour gave me a chance to see how things worked and how I would fit into the team. They already had the likes of Bob Willis and Mark Nicholas calling the game, so I knew I would have some fun talking about cricket with them and maybe taking the mickey along the way.

While I was having plenty of laughs upstairs in the stands, nothing could have been further from the truth out on the pitch, as England continued a miserable run of form that was to last for another decade at least.

And, of course, it was that man Shane Warne who was to be the architect of so much of England's doom.

Now, I don't want to use a fine-tooth comb to go over what was such a terrible time for England in Ashes cricket, because it will only upset me, but it is important to pick out a few performances and matches from that period. I want to draw your attention to a couple of fine English displays in the middle of the mire and also to the performances from the Australians that explain just why they had the edge over us for so long.

In 1994, there was a new captain in the shape of Mark Taylor, who had joined Allan Border's crusade at just the right time and hadn't been scarred by the despair and defeats of the mid-1980s. He brought with him the air of confidence that Australia's revolution needed to keep going. He had to be able to let the free-spirited talents of Michael Slater, Mark Waugh and Shane Warne fly as high as they could, while retaining the hard edge that guys like Steve Waugh and David Boon gave him in spades.

Mike Atherton was in charge of his first Ashes trip and, to be honest, I don't think he knew what had hit him until he got home. The Aussies were completely ruthless and although they won handsomely in both 1989 and 1993, for me this tour was the start of something different. This was the start of the rampant Australia who knew they were good and went about dismantling sides from the word go. There was no room to feel your way into a Test or series; it was wham, bam, thank you, Lamb, Gooch, Gatting and Atherton!

Watching from the sidelines, I was initially frustrated with the way England played and the way they appeared to roll over, but I was convinced it would have taken a natural disaster to stop this Aussie machine when they then went to the West Indies and won a Test series for the first time in 22 years. If anything told us that this Australian team was special, that was it.

The first Test in Brisbane was a brutal affair to begin with. Slats and Mark Waugh went hell for leather with the bat in putting on 182 for the third wicket in a total of 426, both making tons. England really felt the loss of Devon Malcolm, who went down with chicken pox just before the game, especially as he had only just taken 9–57 against the South Africans. You could see how much they missed his pace when Craig McDermott, the old Aussie firebrand, showed he still had a bit of juice in the tank with his six wickets, giving England a mountain to climb.

Even though they had a lead of 259, they refused to enforce the follow-on. This was to become a feature of Australian cricket over the next few years: the desire to win by an innings was less important than just winning. And when you look at their record, who would argue with that? On the odd occasion they did enforce the follow-on, as in the remarkable Calcutta Test match against India in 2001, they actually came unstuck. Personally, I'm a fan of enforcing the follow-on if the bowlers haven't got through too much work in the first innings; it sends out a message of intent. I suppose if you're playing most of your cricket in Australia, the heat factor makes bowling twice in a row much less appealing.

In any case, England were set a completely fanciful target of 508 as Australia went about bowling them out. Somewhat surprisingly, when you think about what subsequently happened, Glenn McGrath was playing against England for the first time and he went completely wicketless over the course of the match. If only that had been the case thereafter. But with so many runs in the bank, Australia didn't need McGrath on that day because they had Shane Warne. Having wowed the world with his Ball of the Century, he became a bona fide Ashes hero in Brisbane by taking 8–71 in 50 overs. That was one heck of a piece of bowling and it told us everything we needed to know about Warne. He was a sorcerer with the ball, spinning it gently or prodigiously depending on his will. Remember, he hadn't suffered any injuries yet, so he could spin the ball furiously. He had complete control of what he was doing, with a four ball being a rarity.

He also showed he had stamina, and not just the sort that lets you run 15 on the bleep test. He had the cricketing stamina to keep wheeling away until he had bowled England out, and that is what you want from your cricketers. Of course, he was a young man back then and when you're young your body will do things for you regardless of your regime, but I wonder if Warney had been born an Englishman and came into cricket now, would they let him play and bowl to his heart's content or would they treat him like Samit Patel and tell him to go away and give up the chips and pizza?

Warney destroyed England in that first Test and, ever the showman, he came as close as I've ever seen anyone come to a hat-trick without actually getting one. He did for Phil DeFreitas round his legs before fizzing in the flipper that completely foxed Martin McCague. Faced with Phil Tufnell, the odds were on a hat-trick, and as Tuffers came forward to what he thought was a big-turning leggie, the wrong 'un spun through the gate and missed the stumps by a coat of lacquer. It was marvellous stuff and for the briefest moment you just watched in wonder as Warney went about his business. If you didn't know he would be a great already, you certainly knew it by the close of that match, in which Australia triumphed by 184 runs.

We had to wait an age for the second Test as the one-day series with Zimbabwe and Australia A got going. I could never understand why there was any need for all the chopping and changing of formats midway through a series. Thank goodness it is all done in blocks these days. When the Christmas Test got under way in Melbourne, England were feeling a bit more confident about things, thanks to a morale-boosting win over Queensland in a three-day warm-up. Gatt hit a double ton before Tuffers collected five wickets to beat a side that included Matthew Hayden, Ian Healy, Stuart Law, Craig McDermott and Andrew Symonds.

That was a rare high point for Tuffers on that trip, during which he was briefly admittted to a psychiatric ward after flipping out and trashing his hotel room following a row over the phone with his second wife. The game is littered with sad stories of men who've cracked either while playing or shortly afterwards, and nothing tests a man's innermost soul more than an Ashes tour. You are helpless with regard to things going on back at home and you're constantly being bombarded by sledging Aussies, so perhaps it is surprising that more men don't lose it out there. In Tuffers' case, he always sailed pretty close to the line. Although he comes across as a Jack the Lad in his post-cricket career, he is quite a sensitive soul, and there was only so much he could take.

Back at the MCG, England's confidence counted for very little as McDermott ripped through them again before Warne put another spell on us. The real story from the game was how Warne made up for coming so close to a hat-trick in Brisbane by getting one with his only three wickets in the second innings. And he had one man to thank for it – Boonie. Now, I've seen Boonie move pretty quickly at times, normally to get to the bar, but the catch he took to dismiss Devon at short leg was nothing but miraculous. Imagine Boonie sat at the table when someone comes along and knocks his VB off the side. He moved so quickly to his right to get a hand under the ball it was as if he was determined not only to catch his beer but not to spill a drop either.

Australia won at an even easier canter this time, by 295 runs, and it was hard to see which way England could turn to get out of their slump. Injuries were playing a part in this series too, with Alec Stewart suffering from a broken index finger, Darren Gough a broken foot and Graeme Hick a slipped disc; Craig White and Shaun Udal both had torn sides, while Athers, Thorpey and Daffy all had problems too. Even the greatest physio of them all, Dave 'Rooster' Roberts, broke a finger when he was pressed into a bit of fielding during the trip.

It was just a nightmare all over. A draw at Sydney meant the Ashes were gone yet again and England could only hope to draw the series. Even that would have been an achievement. And in the dying embers of a magnificent career that included our success in 1986–87, Gatt rolled back the years to score his final Test ton on his final tour in Adelaide as England won the fourth Test to go with the win at the Oval in 1993. There were some trademark Gatting drives in his 117 and those giant forearms were working overtime as he dealt with Warney more easily than anyone had throughout the tour. Even so, England should probably have lost that match too after being reduced to 181–6 in the second innings, which was effectively 115–6, but Daffy had other ideas in his finest moment for England with the bat.

He had simply had enough of being bullied by the Aussies, and in a brilliant session he took the game back to them and showed what happens when they get someone in their face – they don't like it. That was a tactic I used throughout my career to turn situations and games back on them, but no one had done it for a while until Daffy went mad. He took 22 spanking runs from one Craig McDermott over, which reminded me so much of my dust-up with Merv Hughes eight years previously. Every time Craig dropped it short, Daffy pulled him for four until he got so irate and bowled it so short that Daffy could hook it for six!

It gave England something to bowl at, and Devon and Chris Lewis did the damage to secure a 106-run win. England were rightly buoyant, and I can remember that night in Adelaide being great fun. I actually met up with a few of the players who were staying in the same hotel as us, and there was plenty of after-hours drinking that night. But they had earned it.

Of course, the belief that a drawn series would be a formality in Perth came crashing down around everybody's ears when Greg Blewett hit his second ton in his second Test (to go with his first in his first) and a certain G.D. McGrath picked up six wickets in the game, including Athers' twice. It was the start of a beautiful relationship as far as Pigeon was concerned. He'd bowl and Athers would get out and that was it, really. England lost by the biggest margin of the entire tour – 329 runs – and the 3–1 scoreline probably reflected fairly the difference between the sides. They were truly knackered by then too and wanted to come home. I knew that feeling, but it was no excuse for the way they capitulated in the very final innings. To be 27–6 was unforgivable. But then it hadn't been that long ago that the Windies had routed them for 46, so at least there was some consistency.

By the time 1997 came along, England hadn't quite reached rock bottom yet (that would come two years later), but by the end of that summer something became apparent to me. In order for England to win the Ashes back, one of three things had to happen. Either Shane Warne or Glenn McGrath – preferably both – would have to be unavailable to play, England would have to produce some genuinely great players themselves or Australia would have to run out of great players when it came to replacing the likes of Steve and Mark Waugh and Mark Taylor. If none of those three things happened, then I couldn't see how England were going to get the urn back. They were likely always to have pockets of success, as they did at either end of the 1997 summer, because there were some decent players in the side and they would perform sporadically, but the level of skill and consistency that this Australian team had was something different and already they were developing a West Indian air of confidence and dominance that in itself would get them out of tricky situations if need be.

Yet that summer began with something quite remarkable. For the first time since 1989 (and sadly for the last time until 2005), England won an Ashes Test when the urn was actually still at stake. They demolished Australia at Edgbaston, thanks to the bowling of Darren Gough, Andy Caddick and Devon Malcolm, and then backed it up with the knock of his life from . . . it pains me to say this . . . Nasser Hussain. It pains me not as an England fan, which I've always been, but as a good friend and mickey-taking colleague of Nasser's. He knows how hard this is for me to say. Nasser's double hundred, ably supported by Graham Thorpe's ton, was not only a career-defining innings but one that royally entertained the crowd who were lucky enough to watch it. The most entertaining thing that Nasser had done in an England shirt up to that point was to have his fingers broken on a regular basis by the world's fastest bowlers, but in 1997 he was magnificent, and he played the sort of innings we all wish for English batsmen to play.

Victory wasn't guaranteed, despite the 360-run lead, because Aussie captain Mark Taylor chose that moment to save his career with a battling hundred alongside Greg Blewett. The Taylor we saw in 1989 and 1993 was a distant memory by the time he reached English shores as captain for the first time. He hadn't scored a hundred for 18 months and was within a whisker of losing the captaincy, but his Brummie hundred saved him. Still, it didn't save his side from losing by nine wickets and giving England a sense that the rot might finally have stopped.

A draw in a rain-affected Lord's Test suggested that England still had some work to do, and those fears were confirmed three Tests later, with the series and the Ashes nothing but a pipe dream.

Why? Those two meddling bowlers Warne and McGrath. They were the scourge of that summer, with McGrath backing up Steve Waugh's prediction that he would take the series by storm. He ended it with 36 wickets to his name and he opened up a great debate as to whose bunny Athers was. Either his or Curtly Ambrose's, but after McGrath got him seven times in eleven innings that summer, the pendulum had swung the Aussie way, just as it had in world cricket. Old Trafford, Headingley and Trent Bridge all came and went without England taking advantage of the openings they had. If it hadn't been for twin centuries from Steve Waugh in Manchester, things would have been wildly different. By the time Phil Tufnell spun England to glory at the Oval to make the scoreline a respectable 3–2, the game was up, and although the urn remained in the Lord's museum, its spiritual home was now most definitely Oz.

Watching England play Australia had sadly become all too predictable by now. Over the course of the 1998–99 tour, the 2001 series and the 2002–03 tour, Australia won eleven to England's three and, as I've mentioned, each of our wins came when the Ashes was no longer up for grabs, which takes a slight gloss off things. However, winning a single Test match was not easy, so they all meant a great deal.

I was thrilled by England's win at Headingley in 2001 because we got to see Mark Butcher at his very best. Although he didn't hit the heights often enough, he was a batsman I loved to watch when he was in full flow. His 173 not out was an example of what can happen when everything clicks, and I know the feeling. Butch's knock was a classic example of the cricket and the cricketers we had at our disposal in the mid- and late 1990's. Our guys had the talent to perform, but didn't produce it when it really mattered.

That was why Nasser's impact on English cricket when he became captain in 1999 was so profound. He demanded more of players like Butch and Graham Thorpe, and he got it. The wins in Pakistan and Sri Lanka the preceding winter had shown that England were getting better, but when it came to the Ashes, it was the same old story, with the six-wicket win in Leeds the only glimmer of light. I put that series down to the quality of the Australian side more than anything else, though. Adam Gilchrist was behind the stumps and Warne and McGrath continued their double act. I found myself as frustrated as the next Englishman, but, seriously, what can you do when you're up against greatness?

In Australia in 2002, Nasser lost the plot in Brisbane and he knows it. I was out on the ground doing the pitch report and, having played a season at the Gabba for Queensland, I knew the wicket well. It looked like the normal sort of pitch you get there, with a little covering of grass, a hard, true surface perfect for batting. Of course, it would take a bit of turn later on, but this was a bat-first, fill-yer-boots pitch and I told Nass as much. He was in complete agreement with me and had no doubt in his mind what he was going to do, until that coin landed his way up. Only then, at the last second, did he change his mind and make one of the worst calls in Ashes history to stick them in. To this day, he doesn't know why he did it and every time it is mentioned in the Sky box he either leaves the room or just hangs his head in shame, because he knows what an almighty balls-up it was.

If ever a toss set the tone for a series, that was it. By the end of day one, Australia were 364–2, with twin tons from Ricky Ponting and Matthew Hayden, who fell just three short of a double the next day. He made up for it with another ton in the second innings before England collapsed in spectacular style to lose the match by a small matter of 384 runs. Of course, Simon Jones also suffered his horrific knee injury, and you could only feel sorry for him, but that game was already up when Nasser went back into the dressing-room to confirm the bad news. I can even remember looking back to the dressing-room when the call was made to see three England players' heads sticking out of the door as if to say, 'We're doing what?!'

Adelaide saw the birth of something special. It was Michael Vaughan's coming-out party as a batsman of world-class ability. His 177 in the first innings was the sort of display you had got used to watching the Aussies produce, but there he was, with a full head of hair, doing it the English way. It is just a shame he didn't really get more support from his teammates, the next-highest score being 47. Another defeat ensued, leaving Perth as the last chance for England to keep the series alive following seven and a half days' cricket.

The fact that the Ashes were back in Australia's possession after precisely ten and a half days' cricket tells you it didn't exactly go to plan. It was embarrassing, if I'm honest, yet, having watched the previous 13 years of Ashes cricket go more or less the same way, I was getting a little numb to it. England seemed to be able to perform well against the rest of the world, but when it came to Australia we froze. It shouldn't have been like that. If anything, this was the series that should have been bringing the best out of people, but the psychological scars ran deep. That was why Michael Vaughan, Marcus Trescothick, Steve Harmison and Matthew Hoggard were the only players to make it two years later.

At least at Sydney they gave the thousands of fans something to cheer following a 225-run win that avoided the ignominy of a 5–0 whitewash on what was a desperately punishing tour. That match brought Vaughan his third ton of the series and provided some evidence that his remarkable run of form wasn't completely in vain. Little did he know what impact he would have on the Ashes in the future.

ADVANCE, BEEFY FAIR

The beauty of being a commentator is that you get to stay involved with the sport you love without all the extra hassle that goes with it, like feeling knackered and stiff, training in between games and worrying about how well you're going to perform in the next match. My biggest worry these days is which restaurant I'm going to dine in and whether I can get a tee time at my favourite golf courses.

The best thing of the lot is that all the countries I toured as a player have now become open to me in ways I could never have imagined. I had a good time as a player, of that there is no doubt, but now I have the freedom to come and go as I please and get out and actually see the country I'm visiting. We had the odd round of golf as players and were always welcomed by some fantastic hosts to interesting sights, but it is quite difficult to really enjoy those visits when your whole focus is on beating the country you are in.

Now I can use the days in between Test matches to get out and get stuck in to some of my favourite pastimes, like golf and fishing and photography, in some of the most incredible places, and Australia is number one on my list. It is not only home to some of the finest natural surroundings I have seen, it has some of the world's greatest wines and friendliest people. My joy in going to Australia now is two-fold: having the chance to watch England beat them in their own back yard and quaffing their wine while I do it!

There is no better place to experience just that than in Perth, and in particular the Margaret River region. I always associate the area with my good mate Dennis Lillee and he has taught me well about the local produce. First, being on the Western Coast, it has the most fantastic seafood restaurants that I've ever eaten at. One of my favourites is Fraser's, where I ate last tour round with Gus Fraser and pointed out just how he should have upheld the family name. He told me neither this restaurant nor the House of Fraser back at home had anyone who could bowl as well as him, which was a fair point.

In Perth, I met a number of great people, including the late Michael Kailis, who knew I loved fishing and tried to teach me about proper commercial fishing, which was his trade. Unfortunately, I couldn't quite share his passion for that side of things, but he knew a thing or two about the area and the best places to enjoy his produce. He also loved his cricket and whenever I came over he and his family always treated me magnificently. His legacy is a tremendously successful company that also produces cultured pearls, which Kath might have a set or two of.

One man who did teach me a thing or two about fishing was Ken Brown, who owned a boat in Brisbane and has taken me on many a trip to go marlin fishing. I learned almost everything I know about it from him. He also turned Liam into the perfect right-hand man. My son spent about a month living with him back in 1988 during my stint playing for Queensland. I had met Brownie a few years before when I'd chartered his boat and we had become good friends, but when I was living in the Gap for six months with the family, I actually needed him for something else. Liam was spending rather too much time with his mum and his sisters while I was away a lot playing cricket, and I felt he needed a bit more of a masculine influence. Brownie was the perfect man for the job. He was a bit rough around the edges in the way that single-boat skippers are, and Liam loved spending time with him, so we packed him off to live with Brownie a ten-year-old boy and he came back a man . . . sort of.

I made some great mates during my time in Brisbane, with guys like Carl Rackemann and Greg Ritchie in the team, and I always try to catch up with them when I'm back there. Brisbane often gets a bit of a knock because you have to make an effort to find a beach from the city, but I don't think that holds it back at all because the Brisbane River is one of the most stunning you will find weaving through a city, and it has provided me with some of the best city walks I have ever done, ideal training for my charity walks whenever I'm there.

Alongside that training, though, there tends to be at least one wild night out, because my birthday often coincides with the start of the Ashes series and Brisbane has become the traditional opener now. I think e'cco bistro might get another visit from me this year.

When I talk about restaurants in Australia, it is hard for me to look past an old favourite that makes Sydney come alive, in my opinion, and that is the famous Doyles fish-and-chip restaurant in Watson's Bay. It is iconic and always busy, but it is a must-try, and since I first went there in 1978 I've been back each time for more. The thing about heading out there is that you go by water taxi and, for me, that is the best way to get around Sydney. I love the water and I love boats, so jumping into a water taxi to head over to Watson's Bay or Manly or Darling Harbour is a great thing to do. And, of course, it means you get a fantastic view of the Harbour Bridge, which remains such a special landmark. An Englishman might have designed it, but it is quintessentially Australian and every time I see it I know I'm back in my second home.

Round the corner is the Rocks, which has some fantastic bars and restaurants to enjoy, but there is a rich sense of history there too, since it is where many of the first convicts settled, initially in jails and then in homes. You can see some of Sydney's oldest buildings in the area and it just reminds me of why the rivalry between the two countries is so great.

For a lot of people, Sydney becomes their immediate favourite city when they get to Australia, but for a lot of Brits Melbourne is number one because it is said to have a more 'European' feel to it than other Australian cities, and there is some truth in that. For me, Melbourne is a city that has taken time to grow on me, because my first experience there was not a great one. Having come out on a Whitbread cricket scholarship as a youngster, I was ready to fall in love with the place, but one of the wettest summers on record put paid to my cricketing adventure. I was attached to Melbourne University and played about three games in six weeks, which put a real dampener on things, literally. I was so eager to get involved that a lack of cricket ruined my impression of what is really a great city. Subsequent trips there have been much better and I now really look forward to the Christmas period in the city and, of course, the huge event that is the Boxing Day Test. There is no cricket match like it and for me it confirms Melbourne's position as the greatest sporting city in the country, if not the world.

They could fill the MCG with a game of tiddly-winks, they are that sports mad in Melbourne. Whether it is cricket, rugby league, Aussie rules or tennis, they just can't get enough of it. I'm only surprised that it has taken them up until now to get a Super 14 rugby union side there. I've been lucky enough to watch all kinds of sports there, and I must admit that having been taken to a few AFL games by legend and friend Dermot Brereton, I have completely fallen for that sport too.

It can't beat my favourite sport to play these days, though, which is golf. If you're looking for a round, the best courses Australia has to offer are also in Melbourne. The Capital and Royal Melbourne Golf Club are two of the finest courses I have ever played on, and I've played at Augusta. They are just outstandingly beautiful places to play the game, and although I'm not quite a pro – despite what I tell my mate Ian Woosnam – I feel like one when I get to play at places like those.

Again, the Yarra River provides a perfect walking area for me, with the Southbank a real foodie's dream. But if you're looking for a good glass of wine when you're in Melbourne, go no further than the Melbourne Supper Club, a fantastic spot that is hard to find but worth the search.

As a player, I loved playing at the MCG because it was what I felt top-level cricket should be about, with more than 100,000 people watching your every move. It was high-pressure cricket and you had to deliver, and I think that was when I felt most comfortable as a cricketer. The heart would be pumping and you just felt alive.

Nothing has come close to replacing that feeling since.

Most of our cricket was played in the big cities around Australia, but we ventured to one or two outposts as well, and it is fascinating to see how they have grown over the years. We would head for a tour match somewhere like Bundaberg, which was quiet as anything, or even Darwin, which was a very small place when I first visited there in the 1970s, but has grown and developed into a fantastic town. From there, you can really explore the Northern Territory and go to places like the Kakadu National Park.

I actually took my mum and dad up there a few tours ago and we visited Melville Island, just off the coast, and spent a bit of time in the company of the indigenous Aussies. The Aboriginals have an incredible history and the Northern Territory is the perfect place to learn about them, since they have been surviving there for more than 50,000 years. It really is a fascinating place, although some of the wildlife is a little too exotic for me. There are lots of snakes, spiders and crocodiles, none of which would think twice about taking a chunk out of Beefy for dinner. No thanks! I'll have a look, but I'll use my long lens, if it's all the same.

The history of Australia is something I learn a little more about each time I visit and it does help to understand why the desire to beat the Poms on the cricket field is so great. Places like Hobart, huge penal colonies, grew out of English cruelty but have become beautiful places to visit. I don't actually know Hobart as well as I'd like to, but I know that there is a bit more cricket to be played there and I'm intending to get a good look at it this winter.

One place I know I'm going to have yet another good look at is Adelaide in South Australia. That is a place so very, very close to my heart and one that I can't wait to get back to as soon as I have left. It is the kind of big country town that suits a Yeovil country boy like me, and the list of friends that I get to see when I'm there is endless.

I can't fail to mention one very important friend at whose house I always spend Christmas Day before flying back to Melbourne, and that is Geoff Merrill. To think Bob Willis met this king of winemakers in a bar by accident. Bob was having a drink in a bar one evening when he said, 'Jeez, I just can't drink any more of this weasel beer.' Overhearing this, an enormous bloke with a giant moustache sat just next to him turned round and Bob thought he was going to thump him for being rude about Aussie beer. But instead he just said, 'Oh well, don't worry about that, you should come and try our wines!' Bob decided to take him up on his kind offer and Geoff took him to see his vineyard and let him taste some very good wines. He enjoyed it so much that when he went back he got me to come with him. Naturally, being a fan of the grape-related drink, I was keen to get to know more about Geoff and the business, and he was happy to teach me. He loved his cricket and we loved our wines, so inevitably a happy relationship developed and it has continued until this day. So much so that seventeen years after we first met the three of us produced our first bottle of Botham, Merrill and Willis wine, which is going strong, with about seven vintages to date. The wine has done pretty well, but, for us, it is not about making money, just about doing something we all love. Geoff has been our guru of wine and it is a real passion of mine. To be able to produce wine with him has been one of the things I am most proud of in life.

In Adelaide, you will find my favourite restaurant in all the world, and when you look at me you know that I've been into a fair few! It is Georges on Waymouth, and I can think of no better place to have a meal. The food is outstanding and the wine list keeps me occupied all night long. The atmosphere is perfect, while the staff cannot do enough for you. It is simply the best.

The ground at Adelaide is one of the prettiest in the world, a proper cricket ground with character, although as a fast bowler you have to work much too hard for your wickets there these days. At least my days are now spent thinking about what to have at Georges later that evening, which is far less of a worry.

HIGHS AND LOWS

If you can meet with triumph and disaster
And treat those two impostors just the same . . .
Yours is the Earth and everything that's in it,
And – which is more – you'll be a man, my son.

That man is Freddie Flintoff, and his career found its meaning and definition over three Ashes series in 2005, 2006–07 and 2009.

He saw both ends of the spectrum, from national sporting icon to finger-pointed villain and back to hero again before calling it a day. And I don't think it is an exaggeration to say that thanks to him and a fair few other brave Englishmen the Ashes has had new life breathed into it, ensuring that it will stay at the forefront of the game in England and Australia for a long time to come.

Nobody enjoys one-sided contests and for nearly two decades that is exactly what the Ashes became. I think even the Australian public had become a little tired of watching their side dominate for so long, and especially of the way they were going about it. There had been a real backlash over the sledging and the almost arrogant way in which the Aussies had been playing their cricket. A hero was needed to put them back in their place, and who better than Fred to do it?

What you see is what you get with Fred, and back in 2005 he was a cricketer at the peak of his powers. I have known him for a long time and I know the trouble he has had with injuries, going back to the very earliest part of his career, but by 2005 he had put them all behind him to be able both to bat and bowl with complete confidence. Of course, Fred was to have a huge impact on the series, but he wasn't alone. Steve Harmison might have tailed off before he should have done, but he too was at his peak in 2005. He was still on a high from destroying the West Indians in 2004, and he had that dangerous combination that bowlers like Bob Willis and Curtly Ambrose had: pace and bounce; it has been the same since the game began.

Michael Vaughan was in charge and had a calm authority about him that transmitted to the rest of the team, while players like Marcus Trescothick and Matthew Hoggard were ready to fire too. The two men who made all the difference to a side that had started winning 18 months before were Simon Jones and Kevin Pietersen. They were the ones who took England from being a good side to being a great side that summer. I realise some people may disagree with my assertion that the 2005 team was a great side because they did what they did over the course of only one series, but the heights that they scaled during that period are reachable only by greatness, and it was a once-in-a-lifetime series that we must accept was out of the ordinary, so normal rules don't apply.

At the start of the series, I saw a few of the players at various dinners and events, and the atmosphere around the camp was very good indeed. Sometimes you think that the players are trying to convince themselves that things are going well when they're not, but I didn't get that feeling, and there seemed to be a genuine bond between them all. Everyone knew who was in charge and what his own role was; it was just a case of getting the job done on the pitch.

That transmitted to the general public, who were waiting for that series like no other for a generation. During the build-up, I would be stopped in the street more than I had been as a player by people asking me whether England could actually pull off a win. My answer has always been yes, of course they can, but my heart might have been ruling my head in other years. In 2005, though, my answer was an emphatic yes, because that

England team didn't have many scars from previous Ashes campaigns and so weren't afraid of what the Australians had to offer, and they actually wanted to be in the spotlight. It was a really refreshing place to be before an Ashes series and I told Fred simply that he would never have a better chance to beat the Australians. I noticed a change in him in the build-up to the first Test at Lord's. He wanted it so badly that he stopped being the normal relaxed and chatty Fred. He was heading into his shell, and that wasn't him. I thought it was just a few nerves, but his performance in that game didn't match up to the Freddie we had come to expect.

And the truth is that when England lost the first Test by 239 runs, thanks to Glenn McGrath's typical performance at HQ, I was stunned. A lot of people wrote England off, and I can understand why. We had been building up Ashes contests for years only to see them slip away, and it looked like that pattern was set to continue. But a chat with Michael Vaughan following the match convinced me otherwise. Any team can lose a Test match, but a good team rarely loses two on the bounce, and Vaughany was very clear in his mind that he had a good team. I believed him, and I could see it with my own eyes, but we left dinner that night agreeing that if England were to come back, Fred had to get himself back to normal and just play the game he knows.

Edgbaston was five days of pure theatre. From the moment Glenn stepped on a cricket ball to turn his ankle to the moment Geraint Jones caught the final wicket, you couldn't take your eyes off the game. Test match cricket is not supposed to be that exciting, but I can tell you it was ten times more gripping than any 50- or 20-over game that has ever been played.

Finally, it was Australia's turn to make a mistake as Ricky Ponting put us in to bat on a beauty of a pitch and both Tres and Straussy made hay. The way Tres batted was the perfect response to the Lord's defeat because it put England on the front foot and told the Aussies that this team wouldn't lie down. I only felt sorry that Tres didn't get the extra ten runs he needed to get the Ashes hundred he deserved. He never did get one, but this knock was just as important as any ton.

And then there was Fred. Scores of nil and three at Lord's were replaced with a 62-ball 68 that included six fours and five sixes, and all of a sudden he was up and running. That knock fired his summer and proved that confidence is not something you can bottle, but when you have it, you must make the most of it. Three wickets in the first innings helped polish off the Aussies for 308, which gave England a 99-run lead – crucial, since Warney was about to work his magic. Yet again, Fred stood tall to strike 73 and show that he was perfectly capable of playing spin when he didn't have to think about 'the forward press' or some such coaching nonsense. He just played.

Most people will point to the dramatic finish to the game when Steve Harmison had Mike Kasprowicz caught down the leg side as the defining moment of the series, and I'd have to agree, but for sheer drama there was nothing better than the over Fred bowled to get rid of Justin Langer and Ricky Ponting. I don't think I have ever heard a louder crowd at a cricket match in England in my lifetime. It was hairs-on-the-back-of-the-neck time. I think that was when the players on both sides as well as the public knew we had a serious contest on our hands.

The game shouldn't have got as close to the wire as it did, but in the shape of Brett Lee and Warney Australia had two competitors who never knew when they were beaten. It reminded me of Ashes matches of the past and the competitive nature of the men who had gone before. It was as if we were back in 1982 at Melbourne and Jeff Thomson and Allan Border were taking their side crawling over the line. Thankfully, once again England found a solution, and Old Trafford would greet the teams at 1–1.

I have two very vivid memories of the match in Manchester: the sight of thousands of fans being locked out of the gates on day five when the game looked like going down to the wire yet again and the quizzical look on Alex Ferguson's face when he picked up the *Manchester Evening News* just before the start of a new Premiership campaign and realised that football was nowhere near the back page, let alone on it. 'What have your boys done?' he asked me. 'I can't believe there's no mention of any football until about four pages in from the back.'

That was the power of that Ashes series as both teams traded blow for blow, and at Old Trafford it was England in control yet again. This time, it was the captain, Michael Vaughan, who stole the headlines and, unlike in Australia on the previous tour, his giant hundred was not going to be irrelevant. He was masterful in scoring 166 on a quick pitch and it should have been a match-winning ton, but yet again Warney got in the way. Not only did he torment England with the ball but when his side were 133–5 he came in and scored 90 out of nowhere. I know that the only thing he wanted to do as much as be an Aussie rules footballer was score a Test match century, and it was there for him, but even for the man with the best scriptwriter of the lot, some things were just out of reach.

Simon Jones's six-fer meant a 142-run lead, and Andrew Strauss's first Ashes ton gave Vaughany the chance to declare and set about bowling the Aussies out. He just needed to make sure they had enough time.

Standing in England's way was Ricky Ponting – a man who wasn't really used to fighting his way out of a hole like this. But, as a tough Tasmanian, he has that ability preprogrammed into his DNA. His 156 was a great knock and deserved to save his side the game. It showed a side of him that confirmed his status as an all-time great. It is one thing scoring a hundred when your team are in control and your brute of an opening batsman has already bullied the bowlers into submission; it is quite another to bat for seven hours to save a game, and that is what he did – with a little bit of help from one G.D. McGrath.

At this point, England were in the ascendancy, and my chats with the players before games on the outfield and at dinners during the series were now much more relaxed and enjoyable. They all knew they could beat Australia, which is a huge psychological step to take. I don't think any England team between 1993 and 2005 actually believed they could win. They hoped and prayed for a miracle, but this group knew it was possible, and Trent Bridge was the place to secure another piece of history. They still needed a bit of luck to get the job done, but isn't there an old saying about making your own luck? Let's just call that luck Gary Pratt and move on!

For the third match in a row, England hit more than 400 in their first innings, something they hadn't done since the golden summer of 1985, and out in front was Fred, who by now was having the series of his life. He had been in the wickets at Old Trafford and now he was back in the runs, batting beautifully with Geraint Jones as they added 178 before the other Jones came in and demolished the Aussie line-up with some of that newfangled reverse swing.

It had been an awfully long time since England had been in a position to enforce the follow-on in Ashes cricket, so I can only imagine the grin on Vaughany's face when he told Ricky and his mates to strap them on again. He does admit that he wishes he had personally gone into the changing-room and told them, but bearing in mind how Ponting exploded at Duncan Fletcher later that day, perhaps he was wise not to.

Ashley Giles and Hoggy brought the side home in the end after a little wobble in chasing 129. Inevitably, Warney was the one to put a couple of doubts in the mind. But finally England had a 2–1 lead, and even though there was still one Test to go, I never thought the Ashes would be doing anything but coming home.

Kevin Pietersen's ability to rise to the big occasion is the hallmark of a great player and the final Test of that series was made for him. He had relished the chance to play his first one-day games back in South Africa, scoring three hundreds in the process, and what better place to open your Test match ton account than in an Ashes decider at the Oval?

It was a tense affair for England and the players had to dig deep to find a way of keeping Australia at bay. Whether it was Andrew Strauss's 129, Pietersen's 158 or Ashley Giles' career-best 59, men had to stand up and be counted when it mattered, and that was exactly what Fred did in taking only his second-ever five-wicket haul. But it wasn't his five wickets that best represented his achievement in that match; it was his unbroken spell of 18 overs. He just bowled and bowled and bowled, to the point where he was running on pure adrenaline. The Ashes means something to England and to Fred, so if he had to put his body on the line to get them back, that was what he would do on behalf of all of us. He carried the hopes of a nation on his back that summer and he didn't buckle under the pressure. None of the players did, and that is what made it so special.

The draw at the Oval gave England the biggest small prize in the game. Cue wild celebrations, which were just bizarre – but that is another issue. There is a photo of Fred in the dressing-room holding a cigar in one hand and the urn in the other with a broad grin across his face. It sums it all up, all the effort and hard work that went into not only that summer but the previous 18 years. Finally we had our Ashes back. Complete satisfaction is the only way to describe it.

What pleased me most of all was that this was an Australian team that still had Warne, McGrath, Ponting, Hayden, Gilchrist and Langer – all greats of the game, all men who had made life miserable for England over the previous decade, and finally the boot was on the other foot.

I don't believe there is anything more important for an English or Australian cricketer than the Ashes, and I've always believed that, but others try to suggest differently. They thought the 50-over game would kill Test cricket. It didn't. They think the 20-over game will kill Test cricket. It won't. But every now and again we need a reminder why Test cricket is the ultimate. The 2005 series was just that.

My happiness didn't just stem from the fact that England won. It came from watching one of the greatest Test series the world has ever seen. They don't come around that often, but when they do they are the most incredible sporting events around. My only worry is that more and more Test series are just three-match affairs, and that doesn't give enough of a chance for things to ebb and flow. The 2005 matches showed us what the Test game can provide and there is little doubt that it energised Ashes cricket in much the same way that 1981 did.

Why there needed to be an open-top bus parade around London after it, though, was quite beyond me. The players were heroes, they knew it and we knew it, but we took it just a little bit too far in 2005, and if ever a sports team was bitten on their backsides, it was England.

The reason I used Fred to look at the 2005 series is because as happy and as high as he was back then, he was just as low

15 months later as captain on the fateful 5–0 whitewash tour to Oz. It is easy to say with hindsight that he should never have been captain and that giving the captaincy to the team's all-rounder was just asking for history to repeat itself. However, I don't think that is the case. My time as captain of England came relatively early in my career, and perhaps I might have done better had I got the job later. Fred was the stand-out man to do the job, having proved himself on the drawn tour to India. He was the most experienced cricketer at England's disposal. He knew what he was doing and he was the right man to step in for Michael Vaughan.

Where our captaincy careers had a touch of similarity was that our own form deserted us when we needed it most. Lady Luck appeared to be smiling on someone else when we could have done with a cheeky grin now and again. Fred had injury problems to worry about as much as anything else, but the player who could score runs at the drop of a hat in India was no longer on the field in Australia, and that makes life doubly tough for you if you're captain.

The problem with the 2006–07 tour was a lack of preparation, a lack of thought, a lack of respect and a lack of fit and firing cricketers. Even now, thinking about that tour makes my blood boil, because I can accept losing when you give yourself the best chance of doing well and then are beaten by a better team or a quirk of luck or genius. But if you go out to represent your country without giving yourself that proper chance, what's the point? England did not give themselves a fair crack of the whip because they did not get ready for what was a wounded Australian beast ready to act out some revenge. They didn't realise that having won the Ashes once, it was going to be twice as hard to retain them.

Marcus Trescothick's illness at the start of the trip didn't help, but Steve Harmison's total unreadiness for Test cricket was such a let-down. He missed the first warm-up match before the Test with an injury, but it should have been clear to the coaches that he was not prepared for Ashes cricket. He is the sort of bowler who needs to bowl over after over to be ready for action, and without a proper warm-up he was going into the biggest series of the lot cold. No wonder the first ball went straight to second slip. If Nasser Hussain's toss-up in 2002 set the tone for that series, Harmy certainly did the same four years later.

Brisbane was a disaster from start to finish as Ponting clambered to 196 in a total of 602 before McGrath took yet another six-fer to rout us for 157. There was a brief bit of respite when KP and Paul Collingwood both reached the nineties in the second innings, but once they went any chance of saving the game went with them.

It was after that match that I had a chance to spend a bit of time with Fred, who was shell-shocked at what had happened. He takes it to heart when his team doesn't win, and as captain he felt huge responsibility. He insisted things would get better at Adelaide in the next Test. Unfortunately for both Fred and England, that was where the wheels came off the tour.

Things had started brightly enough with Colly and KP picking up where they'd left off in Brisbane to make real contributions. A brilliant 206 for Colly and 158 for KP meant a whopping 551–6 declared and from there England would have been prepared for only two results – either a win or a draw.

Colly's knock was one of the best by an Englishman abroad in living memory. Only six men had scored more than that against Australia in their back yard in the history of the game, and it was so good to watch. His strength through mid-wicket was there for all to see, and, for a diminutive little fella, he stood tall in the face of Brett Lee and Glenn McGrath. That is a feature of Colly through and through – he punches well above his weight and he never takes a backward step. He might not be the most attractive batsman, but he is a hugely effective one and his opponents know they are in a game when they come up against him. Warney's mickey-taking about Colly's MBE for playing in just one of the 2005 Ashes matches wouldn't have bothered him one bit. Engage Colly at your peril, because it will only make him dig in even deeper.

From such a position of strength, England's fortunes turned on a dropped catch by a bloke who I felt should not have even been playing. Nobody drops catches on purpose and it was just one of those things, but Ashley Giles was a patched-up shadow of himself in 2006 and he was the unlucky man to put Ricky Ponting down on 35. Ponting made 142 to get his side up near England's score. What happened next can only be described as pure genius, part of one man's ability to torture a whole nation. Shane Warne captured the wickets of Strauss and Pietersen to send shivers through the England dressing-room, and the team lost it. Wickets tumbled, players were like rabbits in the headlights and, from being in total control, they were bundled out for 129. Australia reached their target of 168 with relative ease.

That was where the tour hit the buffers and it was where Fred needed some support, but it wasn't coming from within the dressing-room. The relationship between Fred and Duncan Fletcher was not great at that stage and the strain was starting to tell. Fletcher knew he needed Fred as an all-rounder to take the game to Australia, but he couldn't really deal with him on a personal level. With their relationship at the top faltering, the strain transmitted through the side and the cracks were starting to tell. There was one last chance to stop the rot at Perth before the Ashes were ripped out of English hands, but it wasn't taken.

Changes were made, with Monty Panesar replacing the injured Giles, and it had an immediate impact as he picked up 5–92 in the first innings. England's batting, however, let them down again. Every single player got caught out. That tells you something about batsman error.

Gilchrist made sure England would be leaving Perth head bowed with an astonishing second-innings attack to bring up his 100 in just 57 balls, and with 557 the target on day three, it was only a matter of when and not if the Ashes would be recaptured. As had been the case so many times, Warney brought the curtain down, taking the final wicket of Monty, and the Ashes, so painstakingly won the year beforehand, was now coughed up in the blink of an eye.

Michael Vaughan, who had been out injured and was watching from the sidelines, was distraught, as were most of the England faithful. I was so angry that those in charge of the England side had thought they could just pitch up and cruise into a Test series with Australia on the back of two thirteen-

or fourteen-a-side warm-up games, rather than proper first-class matches, and keep hold of the Ashes. The whole point of central contracts was supposed to be to make sure that the England squad were well looked after and monitored to ensure they were in great shape for a series like this, but they weren't. There were enough support staff being employed by the EBC, so why couldn't they make sure the players were ready? It is no surprise that they are playing three first-class fixtures ahead of the next tour, because anything less would be a disgrace. I get the feeling that there is no way Andy Flower will allow the same thing that happened four years ago to happen on his watch.

Christmas in Melbourne was a nightmare as the cracks in the side had opened up into wide chasms. Fred was struggling with knee and ankle pain again, but had no choice but to soldier on – and he wanted to. For those of us who saw him in that state, it is no wonder he found a bit of solace in a drink or two. I went out with him on a few occasions and tried to give him all the backing I could, but I was on the outside looking in. I tried to keep his spirits up as a friend and as someone who just wanted to see him and England succeed, but it was a tough time for him, without question.

The innings defeat at Melbourne, where even Andrew Symonds grabbed an Ashes ton, was par for the course by that point, which meant Sydney had to be an English success or the dreaded whitewash would be a permanent stain on the squad.

The fact was that England had been beaten up over four matches and had very little left to give. They were outplayed in each and every department. There wasn't even an exceptional performance from Australia. There were no hundreds, no five-fers, just a decent all-round team display, and that was that. Shane Warne, Glenn McGrath and Justin Langer could all walk off into the sunset as 5–0 Ashes champions. They enjoyed their farewell Tests, Warne in Melbourne and McGrath at Sydney, and I suppose it was all they deserved for years of sterling service, but 5–0 was still hard to take.

What was clear, though, was that Australia's era of complete dominance was over, because I don't care who you've got coming through, you can't replace Shane Warne and Glenn McGrath – you just can't.

For Fred, it was just about the lowest point of his career. He was being pilloried in the media, and unlike in 2005, when he looked behind him and found a team backing him to the full, he was isolated Down Under. The fallout from the Ashes was a slippery slope for Fred that ended up on a pedalo in the West Indies, but it is clear that he wouldn't have batted through the pain of injury and constant defeat if the Ashes hadn't meant so much to him. Sometimes people make mistakes when they are chasing after the things that matter the most to them. It was a lesson learned.

ONE FOR THE FUTURE

Sometimes you have to reach rock bottom before you can start pulling yourself up, and in Ashes terms that was where England had got to in 2006–07. There is no argument that 5–0 was the worst it has ever been for England, but the good news was that it was something that could be fixed.

All the upheaval that followed the defeat, including the loss of two coaches and two captains and an embarrassing defeat to the hapless West Indians in the Caribbean, brought us to 2009 in turmoil but with hope, thanks to the two Andys, Strauss and Flower.

Admittedly, some of the hope was there largely because Australia no longer had most of their legends of the noughties, but there was hope nonetheless. Under Andrew Strauss, England had a team that was certainly going to be prepared, but more than that, they were prepared to fight.

The strange, money-led choice to have Cardiff as the venue for the first Test almost blew up in England's face. The Welsh might love to give us a stuffing in the Six Nations but they put on a decent enough show for the England *and* Wales Cricket Board, and Ricky Ponting loved it. His 150 showed that the Aussies still had one guy capable of exceptional feats. The fact that three of his teammates, Simon Katich, Marcus North and Brad Haddin, all scored hundreds too was a bit more of a concern. England had to survive a final day with eight wickets in hand to leave unscathed. Enter Colly – a man purpose-built for such an occasion – to bat for all but six hours and Monty and Jimmy Anderson to see out the last forty minutes and keep it 0–0. In years gone by, the capitulation would have happened by lunch on the last day, but without Warne and McGrath, who was going to do the damage?

The Ashes had given us another dramatic game. It was a match I will always remember because it was the first time I commentated on a live Ashes Test in England. It had taken a few years to get the rights, but finally Sky Sports was the home of live and exclusive England cricket and we were loving it. There was a spring in the step of every commentator. Warney was set to join us for the second Test, we felt proud to be doing the job and I thought we covered it well.

By the time we got to Lord's, we were up and running and so were England. The boost they got from the draw was much bigger than the disappointment Australia felt at missing out on the win, and they put that to good use in London.

Just as Vaughany had done at Old Trafford in 2005, Andrew Strauss led by example at his favourite ground, with a glorious 161, and that bred confidence from the off. The batting was solid, the bowling of Anderson was impressive and by the time England had batted again the Aussies were the ones fighting to save the game, with a fanciful target of 522 required with two days to play.

Michael Clarke – Australia's next captain – is not quite at the level of a Ponting or a Waugh with the bat, but he's still bloody good, and with Brad Haddin for support he took his side to the close of day four with a glimmer of hope for survival. Cometh the hour, though, cometh the man, and despite constant agony in his knee, Freddie Flintoff rose to the occasion like only he can. Feeling relieved after announcing his Test retirement before the game, he was determined to show the world what it would be missing when he had gone and, more importantly, he was determined to show the Aussies what they would have to get past in order to retain the Ashes.

He bowled ten overs off the reel to take three of the last five wickets and wrap up a first England win over Australia at the ground in seventy-five years. It is just bizarre to think that England have only won six times out of thirty-four against Australia there.

Edgbaston was next. After the drama of 2005, it was unreasonable to expect more of the same, and the rain made sure that it didn't come about. England did enjoy the better of things for the first innings with both bat and ball, but Michael Clarke again got in the way second time around with another hundred.

The real problem for England, however, was that KP needed Achilles surgery and was no longer in the side, while Fred's knee was playing up and was threatening to keep him out of action too.

At Headingley, England learned the hard way that Test matches do not win themselves and that you have to earn the right to dominate the opposition. Flintoff was ruled out by the England management, although he declared himself fit, and that produced the right team selection in his absence but the wrong approach.

Steve Harmison was back and although his recent international form hadn't been great, he always had the ability to make life uncomfortable for the opposition as long as the batsmen had put a few runs on the board. The fact that England were bowled out for 102 was down to pure carelessness. They gave their wickets away and played as if they were batting in Adelaide rather than in Leeds. Even this Australian team weren't going to look a gift horse in the mouth, and with a Marcus North ton setting the platform, their innings victory was more or less a procession.

By this stage, Australia had scored seven hundreds to England's one, but crucially England's bowlers had taken twenty wickets just as many times as the Aussies, and that is what ultimately counts. I've said it before and I'll say it again: bowlers win you matches and batsmen decide by how much.

So to the Oval and a good old-fashioned Ashes decider at 1–1. England need to win and Australia need to survive, so back came Fred for one last hurrah and out went Ravi Bopara, who had been exposed by Australia's bowlers, to be replaced by Jonathan Trott.

Ian Bell was the bit-part player of 2005, but, having come in for the injured Kevin Pietersen at Edgbaston, he silenced his critics with a valuable 72 at the Oval to put England's noses in front, providing the platform on which Stuart Broad could make that lead a length. His 5–37 was simply urn-winning as Australia capitulated for 160.

I had been backing Broad for a couple of years by then because I saw something in him that I liked. There was a fire in him that he clearly got from his dad and he was a character who loved the big occasion. That is always a good starting point, but he also had a lot of skill. Good height, good pace and a great temperament are all you need as a Test fast bowler, and he has all three. Lately, though, I've been disappointed by some unnecessary histrionics and a few too many double teapots when things don't go his way. The player he was in 2009 is the player he needs to remain. If he does that, he will be an England hero many times over.

Jonathan Trott got his career off to a flyer with a maiden Test ton on debut to leave Australia with another rescue job on their hands with two days to bat out. That always seemed unlikely, but anything is possible with Ricky Ponting around.

Fred had not found this game particularly easy due to his ongoing knee problem, but this was his last-ever Test match, and he would have to have crumpled up in a heap before failing to do what he could for his side. The wickets didn't come and nor did the runs, but in a moment of brilliance he effected the run-out of Ricky Ponting with a direct hit that only he could make, thanks to his bullet arm. It was 2005 all over again, only this time Ponting couldn't be upset at the fielder, just at his second Ashes defeat as Australia captain.

An England win showed that the two sides were back on an even keel after the freakish cricketers Australia had produced over the previous 20 years.

If anything teaches us that life goes in circles, it is the Ashes, because no matter how good you think you are, there will always be 11 Englishmen or Australians ready to prove you otherwise. It has been like that for ever, and it will never change.

England will get to go to Australia this winter as Ashes winners and will know that the desire for revenge is burning brightly Down Under, but there will not be a repeat of 2006–07. The Ashes is far too important for that. England have a decent team, as do Australia, and while I don't think we will see the heights of 2005 again, I wouldn't bet against the same result.

Test cricket and the Ashes has got a new lease of life and a whole new legion of fans thanks to the last three series, and I for one cannot wait to see what is in store for us.

As a former Ashes cricketer and an England fan, it still means more to me than any contest I know. I'll take the Ashes over a World Cup, an Olympic gold or a Six Nations Grand Slam. It is history and heritage, it is competition and camaraderie, it is tough and it is skilful and it is joy and pain all rolled into one. It means the world to me and I'd be lost without it. Thank goodness it will always be there.